there with state subsidies supplied the motive power for the trading activities that were the source of Venice's prosperity. Already in the tenth century, a customs official in Pavia had written with amazement, "These people neither plow nor sow, but can buy corn and wine everywhere."

The importance of Venice's mercantile activities in creating a special view of the world cannot be overestimated. Venice had been trading with the Islamic world, as well as with Byzantium, as early as the ninth century, when two Venetian merchants stole the relics of St. Mark from Alexandria. This seminal act inspired the construction of the basilica of San Marco next to the Doge's Palace and marked the beginning of the Venetian state church (FIG. 9). Modeled on the sixth-century Church of the Holy Apostles in Constantinople, San Marco was intended specifically to house the saint's relics. The church would be twice rebuilt, but always on a Byzantine model. Significantly, it was constructed not as a cathedral that would have been under the direct jurisdiction of ecclesiastical authorities, but as the chapel of the doge. As such it was subject to political control, and its proximity to the halls of government laid the groundwork for a close interweaving of the sacred and the secular in Venetian life.

By the end of the twelfth century, the Venetian Republic had consolidated its trading position by establishing permanent colonies on islands throughout the Aegean. These outposts would function in turn as centers for even more rapid expansion after 1204, the year marking the unholy outcome of the Fourth Crusade, when the Venetian navy had joined forces with the French to sack Christian Constantinople. In consequence, San Marco became a display case for political spoils as well as a reliquary for spiritual treasures.

The most visible trophies came from Constantinople. In addition to the bronze *quadriga* (the famous Horses of San Marco) above the main portal on the Piazza San Marco, were a number of objects grouped around the south facade adjacent to the Doge's Palace: two exquisitely carved free-standing marble piers called the pillars of Acri (or the *pilastri acritani*); the four porphyry swordsmen, known as "the Tetrarchs," attached to the corner of the treasury; and the elegant Byzantine reliefs set into the wall above. With the addition of the Pietra del Bando, a truncated column once used for the reading of Genoese colonial decrees and brought back from the

9. View from the Torre del Orologio across the facade of San Marco to the Doge's Palace.

war with Genoa in 1258, the booty offered eloquent testimony to Venice's new commercial hegemony in the east.

By the beginning of the fifteenth century, Venetian galleys were familiar presences in the ports of the Adriatic, the Mediterranean, and the Aegean Seas, and were making regular trips to England, Flanders, and the Black Sea. Many of the major ports and trading cities of the Islamic world – Acre, Alexandria, Cairo, Damascus, Aleppo, Constantinople under the Ottomans – had permanent Venetian colonies or consulates during the Renaissance period.

Accessible to the cities of northern Europe by a number of Alpine passes and to the rest of Italy by the roads and rivers of the great alluvial plain of northern Italy, Venice was also ideally situated to play a significant role in land-based trade within continental Europe. Adventurous Venetian merchants also went further afield. While Marco Polo's *Travels* attested to the opening of the silk route in the thirteenth century, with profitable links established between Europe and the Mongol empire, by the end of the quattrocento we hear from other Venetian travelers who ranged through Persia, Armenia, the Caucasus, and Asia Minor. The patrician Giosafat Barbaro (1413–94) wrote in 1487 that much of this sparsely inhabited terrain, with its diversity of languages, customs, and religions, would still be unknown, "if the mercantile activities and marinership of the Venetians had not opened it up." Ca' Mastelli ("Ca" being the Venetian form of *casa*, or house), built in this period in a traditional Gothic style, was decorated on its canal facade with a bas-relief of a turbanned merchant with a camel carrying on its back a heavy load of merchandise (FIG. 10).

What made Venice different from Genoa and other great seafaring republics was not just the wide-ranging travels of her citizens, but also her central role as entrepôt or emporium to the world. In his *Cronique des Venitiens* (1267–75), Martin da Canal put it in poetic terms, "Merchandise passes through this noble city as water flows through fountains." Even Venetians who never left the confines of the lagoon were continually exposed to the widest range of goods, both exotic and mundane. From Constantinople, whether Christian or Muslim, came a variety of luxury objects; from the Aegean islands came sugar and wine; from the Far East came spices, porcelain, and pearls; from Egypt, the Levant and Asia Minor came gems, mineral dyes, peacock feathers, perfumes, ceramics, alum, and a profusion of textiles – silks, cottons, brocades, and carpets. Germany provided minerals and silver, copper, and iron; from Flanders and England came wool, woven cloth, and tin; from the nearby Dolomites and the Adriatic area came timber; from the Black Sea region came furs, grain, and, regret-

10. Ca' Mastelli, facade on the Rio de la Madonna dell'Orto.

Four statues of Levantine merchants, called *mori*, or moors, are located on the other side of the canal on the Fondamenta dei Mori.

tably, slaves. The list is by no means inclusive. Many of these goods came into Venice only to be shipped elsewhere. And to them should be added such locally made products as glass, patterned silks and other textiles, a variety of crafts and, eventually, printed books. The Venetian eye was – in consequence – practiced and discriminating as to pattern, color, quality, and material.

It was also an eye that appreciated the visual complexity of the pastiche – the collage-like assemblage of "borrowed" fragments – as witness the application of sculptural reliefs to palace facades like those at Ca' Mastelli often without any attempt to integrate them into a coherent design. San Marco itself is a case in point. The trophies displayed on the exterior wall of the treasury are carefully arranged, but in the manner of a miscellany rather than a program. Venetian craftsmen were also master counterfeiters of every sort of artifact and skilled at adapting the lucky find to contemporary use. Many fortuitous acquisitions were incorporated so artfully into the building fabric of San Marco that they look as if they were part of the original design. The elegant gray-veined marble slabs that now line the nave walls were second-hand goods, for example, stripped from the west facade of the church of Hagia Sophia in Constantinople in 1204. About half the six hundred or so columns used in San Marco were imported from Greek lands, and are so well absorbed into the overall scheme that they cannot always be distinguished from the medieval copies.

11. The Pala d'Oro, originally made in 1105 and remade in 1229 and 1345. Gold altar screen, with 255 *cloisonné* enamels and 1,927 pearls and precious stones, 10'11½" x 6'11½" (3.3 x 2.1 m). San Marco, Venice.

The stones include garnets, emeralds, sapphires, amethysts, rubies, agates, topazes, carnelians, and jasper.

Inside San Marco the renowned Pala d'Oro, a sumptuous gold altarpiece encrusted with jewel-like enamels and precious gems, was itself a pastiche (FIG. 11). Probably the single most precious object in the basilica, it was originally ordered from a Constantinopolitan workshop by a tenth-century doge. It was remade in Venice at least twice, with the Byzantine enamels and jewels reset in a new Gothic frame in 1345. The total effect is one of dazzling richness and exotic intricacy: qualities perfectly suited to an ever more refined aesthetic taste.

An even more telling example of Venetian adaptation is an intriguing object inside the treasury of San Marco, known as the "Grotto of the Virgin" (FIG. 12). Its manufacture must have begun when an unknown Venetian artisan was presented with a piece of rock-crystal, probably late-antique booty from the Fourth Crusade. Carved into the shape of a central-plan building, the

yet, the viewer of a mosaic is always aware of the material substance of the medium and the fact that the surface is there and tangibly present. It is not just a transparent window into another world behind the surface; this sense of the built-up surface would also carry through into Venetian Renaissance painting.

The influence of the mosaics was not just visual and passive in nature, for Renaissance artists were continually involved with them in a very real physical sense as they restored or even replaced them with their own designs. Christ in Majesty in the semi-dome of the main apse, for example, was created in 1506 by a Master Pietro who sought, albeit in the middle of the High Renaissance, to replicate archaeologically the venerable Byzantine prototype of the twelfth century. And yet the same artist also made a mosaic of St. Matthew the Evangelist, just visible to the right in the southeast pendentive of the presbytery dome (see FIG. 13), in a full-blown Renaissance style. Better known artists, such as Titian, Veronese, Tintoretto, and Palma il Giovane, also eagerly contributed their own cartoons to "restore" the medieval mosaics in an up-to-date manner.

Just as the mosaics themselves were restored, replaced, and added to by artists over the centuries, so too successive generations would look into the basilica with new eyes and draw from them varying messages to meet new concerns and challenges. The stylistic evolution of the Venetian altarpiece demonstrates the power and mutability of the Byzantine example. In the trecento it

15. PAOLO DA VENEZIA
S. Chiara Polyptych,
c. 1350. Panel, 5′5¾ x 9′4″
(1.7 x 2.9 m). Gallerie
dell'Accademia, Venice.

The tiny figure of a
Franciscan nun, the
probable patroness of the
work, appears in the *Death
of St. Francis*, in the second
pinnacle from the right.
The sun and moon beneath
Mary's feet allude to John
the Evangelist's vision of the
Woman of the Apocalypse
in Revelations 12:1.

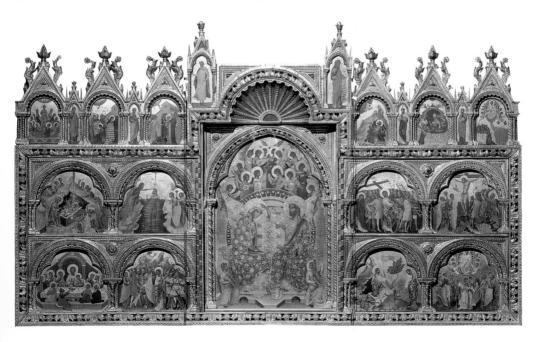

was the golden refulgence, the brilliant vitreous color, and the material preciousness of the mosaics that inspired Paolo da Venezia (c. 1290–1358/62). The earliest Venetian painter known to us as an artistic personality, he introduced the compartmented polyptych, a type that would become the norm in Venice (FIG. 15). Paolo combined Byzantine and Gothic elements in his sumptuous S. Chiara Polyptych in an idiosyncratic, but convincing, new synthesis. Painted in a miniaturist technique based upon the minute observation of tiny details that is reminiscent of the Pala d'Oro, the ensemble looks from a distance like an intricate tapestry. The large central panel features the Coronation of the Virgin, originally a French iconographical theme, with Christ and the Virgin sharing a double throne and serenaded by a choir of music-making angels. The spiritual and physical center of the ensemble, the coronation panel is framed by scenes from the lives of Christ and St. Francis. The luxury fabrics worn by the holy figures feature a range of silks embroidered with floral patterns found on Chinese silks and ceramics and offer compelling circumstantial evidence of Venice's trade with the Far East. Brilliant color, used with characteristic Venetian subtlety and restraint, is transformed in the manner of mosaics or the Pala d'Oro into a rich chromatic harmony by means of the unifying matrix of the gold background.

In the quattrocento the ornamental values of the San Marco mosaics still appealed to Venetian artists, but now they were to be reinterpreted according to new standards of naturalism. Giovanni Bellini (c. 1430–1516) was able to satisfy both demands with yet another novel synthesis in a succession of altarpieces culminating in the S. Zaccaria *pala* of 1505 (FIG. 16). Few artists still used gold leaf for the backgrounds of their altarpieces, for in an age that increasingly prized pictorial realism, the holy figures were supposed to be placed in a credible physi-

16.   GIOVANNI BELLINI
S. Zaccaria Altarpiece, 1505. Canvas transferred from wood, 16'5" x 7'8½" (5.0 x 2.4 m). S. Zaccaria, Venice.

The Madonna and Child are flanked by SS. Peter and Catherine, Lucy and Jerome. The connection of Bellini's painted apse with the marble frame would have been more apparent before the painting was cut into a rectangle.

20. Ascension dome (bottom); Holy Women at the Sepulchre (west vault); and Pentecost dome (top). Mosaic, 12th century. San Marco, Venice.

The Pentecost dome symbolizes the institution of the Church and the descent of the Holy Spirit after Christ's Ascension. The twelve apostles, filled with the Holy Spirit that radiates from the dove displayed in the throne at the center of the dome, receive the gift of speaking in foreign tongues and are inspired to preach the Christian message to all the nations of the world (represented by the paired figures situated between the windows at the base of the dome; see FIG. 14, page 28).

21. Vittore Carpaccio
Healing of the Possessed Man, 1494 (detail). Canvas, whole work 11′11¾″ x 12′9″ (3.7 x 3.9 m). Gallerie dell'Accademia, Venice.

foreigners, to mariners, shipyard workers, and unskilled laborers – this too was a social category and not an economic class.

By the end of the quattrocento, trading activities and immigration resulting from the westward advance of the Turkish empire, had produced one of the most heterogeneous populations in Europe. The *calli* and *campi*, Venetian dialect for streets and public squares, were so full of exotically clad visitors and immigrants – among them Germans, Slavs, Albanians, Dalmatians, Turks, Mamluks, Arabs, Africans, Persians, Greeks, and Levantine, German, and Spanish Jews – that one visitor remarked of the city, "Most of their people are foreigners" (FIG. 21). This motley crowd, while con-

With its luminous color, exquisitely detailed landscape, incisive portrayals, and semblance of movement, Dürer's *Feast of the Rosegarlands* was a dazzling *tour de force*. All Venice, including the doge and the patriarch, flocked to see it. Never one to suffer from false modesty, Dürer wrote to Pirckheimer that "there is no better image of the Virgin in the country."

And yet Dürer's situation in Venice was ambiguous. The admiration that he earned from the aristocracy was matched by resentment from the artists, not all of whom were as self-confident as Giovanni Bellini. Early in his stay, Dürer had confided to Pirckheimer, "Amongst the Italians I have many good friends who warn me not to eat and drink with their painters. Many of them are my enemies and they copy my work in the churches and whenever they can find it, and then they revile it and say that the style is not 'antique' and so not good." Several months later Dürer complained further: "The painters here, let me tell you, are very unfriendly to me. They have summoned me three times before the magistrates, and I have had to pay 4 florins to their Scuola." Dürer, for all his distinguished reputation, had run head on into the tightly regulated world of the Venetian guilds.

The World of the Guilds

While the making of art throughout Europe in this period was admittedly more a commercial business than a vehicle for self-expression, its mercantile nature was particularly notable in Venice. Like virtually every other trade practiced in the city, the arts were protected and controlled by the state. Architects and sculptors who

worked in stone were required to join the Arte dei Tagliapietra, or stonemasons guild (FIG. 24), while woodcarvers formed their own group, the Arte dei Intagliadori. But the Arte dei Depentori, whose statutes dating to 1271 make it the oldest known painters' guild in Italy, was all-inclusive. By the end of the sixteenth century, its membership was divided into eight categories, called *colonelli*. These included not only the figure painters and illuminators whom we would now define as true and proper artists, but also gilders, textile designers and embroiderers, artisans of gold-tooled leather, playing-card makers, mask makers, and sign painters.

This inclusiveness encouraged two important tendencies. In the first place it tended to level the genres, with no official hierarchy or division between crafts carried out by artisans and the "fine arts," the prerogative of the artist. In consequence, it took considerably longer in Venice than in some other centers for figure painting to be considered a liberal art: only in 1682, a good century later than their counterparts in Florence, did Venetian painters split off and form their own guild, the Collegio dei Pittori. In the second place, while individual painters might work in several of the fields recognized by the guild, with major artists from Paolo da Venezia in the 1300s to Titian in the 1500s involved in such craft-like activities as festival decoration, mosaic design, and banner making, they were strongly discouraged from crossing media boundaries into sculpture. Court records suggest that territorial disputes were common, with carvers and painters each jealously guarding (though not always successfully) the exclusive right to practice their crafts.

The guilds were involved in the lives of artisans in a number of ways. One of their functions was political, an aspect that would have been clear to each member of a guild from the moment that he was sworn in and had to pledge his allegiance to the doge. Back in 1310 the officers of the painters' guild had been presented with a unique opportunity to prove their loyalty by helping to quash one of the few rebellions in the republic's history. Led by a patrician, Baiamonte Tiepolo, it was quickly put down when the painters joined with several members of the Scuola di S. Maria della Carità to capture the fleeing rebels in a pitched battle in the Campo S. Luca. The patriotic deed was commemorated with a flagpole base, carved with the emblems of each *scuola*, that stands in the *campo* to this day.

Guilds also played a special civic role on occasions of ceremony and celebration. Twice a year, on the feast days of St. Mark and Corpus Christi, guild members displayed their corporate identities to the city at large in the spectacular processions that wound

Disegno Della Sens
a Antica Di Venezia

25. GABRIELE BELLA
*The Ancient Feast of the
Sensa*, c. 1790. Oil on
canvas, 38¹/₂ x 58¹/₂″ (98 x
148.5 cm). Pinacoteca della
Querini Stampalia, Venice.

around Piazza San Marco. Many of the trades concerned with the production and sale of luxury items – paintings, furniture, textiles, carpets, mirrors and objects of glass, gold, and silver – displayed their wares on holidays, when shops were ordered to remain closed. The most famous such event was the annual Feast of the Sensa, a fifteen-day fair that culminated in the ancient ritual of the Marriage to the Sea on Ascension Day in which the doge's – and thus Venice's – lordship of the sea was reaffirmed each year. A kaleidoscopic array of imported and locally made merchandise was displayed in a motley assortment of improvised *botteghe* (stalls) and handcarts which filled Piazza San Marco (FIG. 25). It was the only time during the year that foreign artists were allowed to sell their pictures in Venice without incurring fines such as those

26. BARTOLOMEO VIVARINI
St. Ambrose Altarpiece,
(central panel), 1477. Panel,
49¼ x 18½" (125 x 47 cm).
Gallerie dell'Accademia,
Venice.

levied on Dürer. The event attracted crowds of visitors from near and far.

Artisans also played a role in extraordinary demonstrations, such as the festivities that followed a Venetian naval victory over the Turkish fleet at Lepanto in 1571. Upon this occasion, the drapers' guild bedecked the Rialto bridge with canopies and lanterns and festooned the sides with colorful bunting. The painters' guild then further embellished the structure by using the fabrics as a backdrop to display canvases by their most illustrious members, past and present, including Giovanni Bellini, Giorgione, Pordenone, Titian, and Jacopo Bassano.

It is worth noting, however, that the Venetian guilds, unlike many of their counterparts in Florence and other cities, never wielded any real political authority. In Venice, a sense of participation and a rhetoric of inclusion provided an effective substitute for the exercise of power.

Indeed, the Venetian guilds were primarily concerned with the day-to-day practice of the trade, and their greatest impact on the lives of artisans was in the economic sphere. The guild restricted the number of apprentices allowed to enter the trade; it established norms for training, apprenticeship, and promotion to journeyman status – for sculptors, upon presentation of a *base attica* (a classical base), for painters, *un anchona a più colori* (an altarpiece in many colors); it defined days and hours of work; it set quality control standards for the various objects made by guild members; it appointed peer juries to appraise completed works; it oversaw contractual agreements. All such rules were designed to level the playing field amongst Venetian artists of an acceptable level of competence, but of vastly different levels of skill and creativity. They were also intended to give those artists – and the economy of the city – every advantage over outside competition.

The social and religious aspects of an artisan's life were centered in the *scuola* that was attached to each trade guild. As with the other *scuole*, those based upon occupational groupings functioned like miniature commonwealths. Each included a broad spectrum of members, from the most prosperous master of a busy workshop to the humblest apprentice who was still grinding pigments and sweeping the floor. The members elected officers

ach year, attended regular meetings, and wor-
hipped together. They buried the dead, dow-
red their daughters, and assisted each other in
imes of illness or economic hardship. Like many
of the *scuole*, the Scuola dei Pittori operated its own
mall hospital.

Each *scuola* maintained an altar in a parish church
or, if particularly wealthy, its own meeting house. In
ither case, decorative embellishment was not only
itting, it was necessary for the honor of the group.
The stonemasons, who had an altar in the church
of S. Aponal, commissioned a polyptych from Bar-
olomeo Vivarini (c. 1432–91) in 1477. According
o an inscription on the work, at least two of the five
oly figures depicted, Ambrose and Peter, were the
ame saints of the *gastaldo* and the *scrivan*, the chief
fficers of the *scuola* at the time. Their financial con-
ribution to the commission, as well as those of other
nembers, was also acknowledged by their inclusion
n the group of worshippers who kneel at the feet
of St. Ambrose in the central panel (FIG. 26). The
mage of collective piety is emblematic of confraternal ideals of
olidarity and cooperation.

The Scuola dei Pittori met in the church of S. Luca, their patron
aint, until 1532 when a substantial bequest left by one of their
members, Vincenzo Catena, allowed them to build their own meeting house near S. Sofia. The building has long since been put
o other use, but the door jambs still exhibit reliefs of St. Luke the
Evangelist as emblems of the *scuola* (FIG. 27).

As Dürer learned to his annoyance, special sanctions were
mposed by the guild on foreign artists who made and sold objects
in Venice. Even if he had become a permanent resident of the city
and thus eligible to join the painters' guild, his entrance fee would
still have been double that required of a native artist, and he could
normally sell his works only in his shop and not any other place.

The protectionist policies of the guild were aimed at main-
taining an exclusive caste. The position of the government, as indi-
cated by Dürer's popularity with the patrician ruling elite, was
rather different. On the one hand, exports were to be encouraged
and imports discouraged for the sake of the local economy. Heavy
duties were accordingly levied on imported altarpieces, and standards relaxed on those made for the export market. Special dis-
pensations were sometimes granted to further particular economic
goals. The painters were thus allowed by the government to work

27. *St. Luke the Evangelist*,
1572. Istrian stone relief,
8⅓ x 13″ (21 x 33 cm).
Capital of corner pilaster on
the entrance to the former
Scuola dei Pittori, Strada
Nova, Cannaregio
4186–4190, Venice.

Accompanied by the bull,
his traditional attribute, St.
Luke is depicted in the act
of painting. The *scuola*
premises were located on
the *piano nobile*, the floor
above the retail shops on
the ground floor. Early
accounts describe exterior
walls covered with fresco
decoration and an interior
filled with paintings by the
group's most distinguished
members. The Cannaregio is
one of the largest *sestiere*, or
districts, of Venice.

The Making of a Visual World

Allegory of Time Governed by Prudence, c. 1565. Oil on canvas, 30 x 27" (76.2 x 68.6 cm). National Gallery, London.

The portraits represent the Three Ages of Man. Titian reinforces the metaphor by moving from smooth brushstrokes and full illumination for the young Marco to an impressionistic application of paint for his own portrait, which seems to dissolve into the shadows. The three animal heads symbolize Prudence, a hieroglyph based upon the writings of Macrobius (5th century AD). While the wolf beneath Titian represents the past that devours memory, the lion, strong and fervent, stands for the present which acts, and the dog stands for the future which flatters. An inscription in Latin above the figures completes the allegory: "From the past, the present acts prudently, lest it destroy future action."

nd was the artist responsible for completing Titian's *Pietà* (see IG. 17, page 32). That Titian, himself a brother of a painter, thought of his successors in dynastic terms is suggested by his *Allegory of Time Governed by Prudence* (FIG. 36). In it he portrays himself, along with his son Orazio (1525–76) and young nephew, Marco 1545–1611), who were also painters. After the death of Paolo Veronese, the artist's brother Benedetto Caliari (1538–1598) and ons Carletto (1570–96) and Gabriele (1568–1631) carried on the amily tradition and signed their paintings *eredi di Paolo* (heirs of Paolo).

Jacopo Robusti, called Tintoretto (1518–94), had a large family and a busy workshop. His three principal assistants were his ons Domenico (c. 1560–1635) and Marco (died c. 1637), and his daughter Marietta (c. 1556–c. 1590). In his will, Jacopo asked his on Domenico to complete those works still unfinished at the time of his death and ordered that all the drawings, plaster casts, models and other things pertaining to the workshop be kept together in the family business. His daughter Ottavia helped to perpetuate the enterprise in another way. In her will of 1645 she wrote that she had promised her brothers that she would marry Sebastian Casser, a German employed in the workshop, "if he proved to be an able painter . . ." She further explained, "In this way, by virtue of his talent, the Tintoretto name would be maintained."

The Artist as Individual

While family businesses ensured continuity, they also had the potential of stifling individual creativity. And yet, for all the emphasis on cooperative ventures, Venetian artists were not absent from the debates of the period on the nature of artistic genius. A humanist poet at the court of Ferrara thus addressed a sonnet to Jacopo Bellini in 1441: "How you may exult, Bellino, that what your lucid intellect feels, your industrious hand shapes into rich and unusual form. So that to all others you teach the true way of the divine Apelles and the noble Polycleitus; because if nature made you perfect, that is a gift from heaven and your destiny." Not averse to such notions, Jacopo did not hesitate to add an inscription to a *Madonna and Child* in 1448 that affirmed, HAS DEDIT INGENUA BELINUS MENTE FIGURAS (Bellini produced these forms with his genius).

Ten years later, the medallist Zuan Boldù (active 1454–d. before 1477) used a different medium to express a heightened sense of the artistic self (FIGS 37 and 38). He depicts himself on the obverse of his portrait medallion in a resolutely classical manner, with shoulders heroically nude and curly hair bound with an ivy-leaf wreath. On the reverse of the medal Boldù offers a personal meditation on death and immortality. Now depicting himself as a full-length figure who clutches his head in an attitude of despair, the artist participates in his own allegory. To his right, a winged putto rests on a human skull and holds a flame in his left hand. The putto and skull symbolize the inevitability of physical death, while the flame alludes to the possibility of immortality through the ineffable permanence of fame. The artist confirms not only his identity, but also his proficiency in classical languages – the mark of a good humanistic education – with the same inscription on each side of the medal, on the obverse in Greek, on the reverse in Latin, "Ioannis Boldù Painter of Venice."

Below and opposite above
37 and 38. ZUAN BOLDÙ *Self-Portrait* (obverse) and *Allegory of Death* (reverse), 1458. Bronze, diameter 3$\frac{1}{3}$" (8.5 cm). Museo Civico Correr, Venice.

By the end of the century most Venetian artists were latinizing their names to give themselves classical roots. Vetor Scarpazza (known to us as Vittore Carpaccio) became Victor Carpathius; Giovanni Bellini signed himself Ioannes Bellinvs; and Lorenzo Lotto was now to be Lavrentivs Lotvs.

Ten years later again, Giovanni Bellini used the authority of the classics to call attention to his own gifts with a graceful paraphrase from the ancient Roman poet Propertius. Inscribing it on a *cartellino* (or little card) in the Brera *Pietà* (see FIG. 35, page 56), he alludes to the superior ability of the painter to invoke a living presence that would inspire empathy in the spectator: *HAEC FERE QVVM GEMITVS TVRGENTIA LVMINA PROMANT BELLINI POTERAT FLERE IOANNIS OPVS* (When these swelling eyes evoke groans, this very work of Giovanni Bellini could shed tears). That the *cartellino* is itself an artifice – a fictive scrap of paper seemingly pasted to the sarcophagus – suggests also that painting is superior to writing in the imitation of reality.

Bellini was making a *paragone*, a popular intellectual game that Renaissance humanists had picked up from classical texts. It involved an argument over the respective worthiness of two or more arts and most often centered on a comparison of painting with poetry, such as that made by Bellini, or of painting with sculpture.

Just as Boldù had celebrated his humanist credentials with his portrait medal, other artists employed their artistic skills to define their place in the social order. As an officer of the Scuola Grande di S. Marco, Gentile Bellini was able to paint his portrait into his *St. Mark Preaching in Alexandria* along with those of his confraternity brothers without offending the collective mentality (FIG. 39). But he did not hesitate to accouter himself with a red toga as well as the golden chain of knighthood that had been bestowed upon him in 1479 by the Ottoman sultan Mehmed II.

By the end of the century, the humanist Francesco Negro would praise the Bellini brothers: Gentile for his mastery of the theory, and Giovanni for the practice, of painting. Commending the two artists as models of right living, Negro defined painting as a genteel occupation befitting patrician youth: "the remedy for excessive study and no less an approach to virtue and an honorable relaxation of the mind and the body." Such ideas, based upon precedents in classical literature, were commonplaces in humanist writings on art.

For all the praise of the Bellini by poets and humanists, however, the painters remained essentially men of the workshop. Most of their works were made to serve specific functions – political, religious, didactic – in specific sites. With the work of Giovanni

39. Gentile Bellini
St. Mark Preaching in Alexandria, 1507 (detail). Oil on canvas, whole work 11'4½" x 25'3" (3.5 x 7.7 m).
Pinacoteca di Brera, Milan.

Evidence of a widespread fascination with Egyptian lore, the hieroglyphs on the obelisk directly above the head
of St. Mark are Renaissance inventions. Humanists saw the pictograms not only as a key to the mysteries of the
ancients, but also as a universal language that could express any idea or metaphysical concept, at least to the initia

Bellini's pupil Giorgione, however, we find the beginnings of a new genre of cabinet paintings, generally smaller works made solely for the enjoyment of a new category of patron: the art collector. We also find an engagement of the artist himself in literary and philosophical circles. It was Giorgione who provided the visual realization of the Arcadian world that Pietro Bembo (1470–1547) evoked in *Gli Asolani*, a collection of platonic dialogues on love that were set in the countryside near Asolo. According to Vasari, writing some fifty years after the fact, the "gentle and courteous" Giorgione was "always a very amorous man and he was extremely fond of the lute, which he played so beautifully to accompany his own singing that his services were often used at music recitals and social gatherings." Whether or not Vasari's account can be trusted in all its particulars is not the point; for it reveals to us a new romantic view of the artist who is more than just a maker of art, but has now become a personality in his own right.

Giorgione's early death cut short an already legendary career. An artist of surpassing originality, he laid out the parameters of cinquecento painting in Venice, just as Jacopo Bellini had done it for the generation that preceded him. It was, however, Giorgione's successor Titian who would achieve an unprecedented international fame and clientele that rivaled even Michelangelo.

Spanning three-quarters of a century, Titian's career was characterized by a continuous upward trajectory of achievement and success. Named a Count Palatine and Knight of the Golden Spur by the Holy Roman Emperor Charles V in 1533, who also appointed him as his official court artist, Titian was now both a painter and a gentleman. He was also one of the first artists whose reputations would be crafted by the writings of contemporary critics. As such, he came to embody Venetian painting in the great aesthetic debates of the sixteenth century.

Making direct analogies between Titian's brush and his own pen, the writer Pietro Aretino (1492–1556) fired a familiar salvo in the *paragone* debate when he praised Titian's ability to rival nature. But the imitative skill that Aretino saw as a virtue was a threat to the Tuscan conception of painting which valued the intellectual over the sensual. Vasari thus criticized Venetian artists, even Titian whom he grudgingly admired. Their shortcoming lay in their insistence on privileging the sensuous act of *colorito* (the application of colors) over the intellectual process of *buon disegno* (good design: draftsmanship from idea to drawing) as the fundamental component among the three essential constituents of painting: *invenzione, disegno, colorito* (invention, design, coloring). It was

DEL S TITIANO PITTORE.

Molti in diuerse età dotti Pittori,
Continuando infino a tempi nostri,
Han dimostro in disegni e bei colori
Quanto con la natura l'arte giostri:

E giunti furo al sommo de gli honori,
E tenuti fra noi celesti Mostri.
Ma TITIAN, merce d alta uentura,
Vinto ha l'arte, l'ingegno, e la Natura.

40. Titian's *impresa*, from Battista Pittoni, *Imprese di diversi prencipi, duchi, signori, e d'altri personaggi et huomini letterati et illustri . . . Con alcune stanze del Dolce che dichiarano i motti di esse imprese*, 1568, no. XXXXIII. Private collection.

The verse below the *impresa*, written by Ludovico Dolce, states that art has competed with nature throughout the ages, but that Titian has triumphed over art, genius, and nature.

disegno, Vasari held, that offered the means to elevate art above the order of nature. Measurable, rational, and concrete, *disegno* was also the father of all the arts: painting, architecture, and sculpture.

Taking the Venetian side in what has come to be called the *disegno-colorito* controversy, Ludovico Dolce (1508–68) praised Titian for those very transgressions that had so perturbed Vasari. It was probably Dolce or Aretino who had thought up a personal *impresa* (a heraldic device and motto) for the artist (FIG. 40). It consists of an image of a she-bear licking her cub into shape and the motto: NATURA POTENTIOR ARS (Art more powerful than nature). Referring to a simile applied by classical writers to the poetry of Virgil, the device implied that the bear's offspring were born without form and had to be shaped in this way by their mother. The analogy to the artist, as well as to the poet, was obvious. He too gave form to raw material and, licking it into shape, improved on nature.

A member of the Arte dei Depentori to the end of his life, Titian was still very much a man of business, providing his patrons with products of unassailable quality. His talent, intelligence, and self-confidence gave him more latitude than most of his peers, but it cannot be argued that he engaged in "art for art's sake." In a final self-portrait painted near the end of his life, he summed up the delicate balance of art and craft that had allowed him to transcend the boundaries of caste in an ever more rigid society (FIG. 41). The heavy gold chain of honor bestowed upon him by the emperor is just visible as a subtle statement of rank, but in his hand he holds a brush, the tool of the painter's trade.

Titian's dazzling preeminence should not blind us to the sheer quantity of artistic talent in Venice during the Renaissance period. The making of a visual world is the product of a broad collaboration, knowing and unknowing, between artists of every level of skill, patrons across the economic and social spectrum, and viewers of every quality and condition.

Titian's *Battle of Spoleto*, a skirmish between the papal and the imperial armies, is partly known to us from his own preparatory drawings and several copies by other artists (FIG. 47). Attesting to Titian's achievements as a history painter of great dramatic power, these chance survivals offer a more complete vision of an artist whose greatest surviving works are primarily religious subjects, portraits, and mythologies. Set against the backdrop of a mountainous landscape studded with burning buildings, the action develops with a counter-clockwise movement around a stone bridge spanning the river in the foreground. The emperor's troops, mounted on horseback and wearing contemporary armor, gallop in from the right. Crossing the bridge, they savagely put to rout the papal army, clad in *all'antica* (antique style) armor, who try to hold their ground on the opposite side.

Titian was aware of artistic developments in central Italy and almost certainly gained ideas from the frescoes planned for the Palazzo Vecchio of Florence at the beginning of the century. Michelangelo's cartoon for the *Battle of Cascina* had never been executed, but Titian's rendering of the human body in contorted poses and violent action is good evidence that a copy of it had reached Venice by the 1530s. Likewise, the rearing horses on the bridge suggest an awareness of Leonardo's *Fight for the Standard*. The only part of his *Battle of Anghiari* to be completed, it would have been visible until it was painted over by Vasari in the 1560s.

47. TITIAN
Battle of Spoleto, c. 1537. Black chalk with white highlights and traces of brown wash on blue squared paper, 15 x 17½" (38.3 x 44.6 cm). Louvre, Paris.

The work has also been identified as the *Battle of Cadore*. The early cycle was begun by Gentile and Giovanni Bellini in 1474 as a replacement for a fresco program begun by Guariento in the middle of the fourteenth century.

The new abbreviated version of the cycle that was installed in the Great Council Hall in the 1580s after the fire is emblematic of long cherished Venetian attitudes about civic art. In the first place, the twelve paintings that comprise it exhibit a striking stylistic unity, considering the involvement of twelve artists of varying degrees of talent and skill. The traditional Venetian emphasis on consensus and cooperation was clearly operative in the collective workshop. Secondly, in accordance with the documentary status accorded history paintings in Venice – they were often cited as forms of visual proof – the new works almost certainly replicated in a general way the compositions that they replaced. Titian's battle was not one of the subjects that was repeated, but Francesco Bassano's (c. 1540–92) *Consignment of the Sword* (FIG. 48) restored a subject painted by Gentile Bellini in the late fifteenth century. Bassano's composition is strikingly close to Vasari's account of the earlier version of the work. Describing an episode where Doge Sebastiano Ziani is about to lead the Venetian army into battle with the emperor on behalf of the pope, Vasari wrote: "One sees the Pope, standing in pontifical dress, giving the benediction to the Doge, who armed and with many soldiers behind him, prepares to go to the enterprise. Behind this Doge one sees infinite

48. FRANCESCO BASSANO
*Consignment of the Sword
by the Pope to the Doge,*
1584–87. Oil on canvas,
18′4¹/₂″ x 18′4¹/₂″ (5.6 x
5.6 m). Great Council Hall,
Doge's Palace, Venice.

49. JACOPO PALMA
IL GIOVANE
*Allegory of the League of
Cambrai*, 1590–95. Oil on
canvas, 12'10¾" x 15'2"
(3.9 x 4.6 m). Senate Hall,
Doge's Palace, Venice.

Vasari had seen the larger picture, but he may have missed
the point. To Venetian eyes, the granting of the sword, an emblem
of sovereignty and just rule, would have been the conceptual heart
of the scene. Bassano, on his part, embeds the episode within
the bustle and circumstance of a festive occasion on the *molo* (water-
front) of the Piazzetta: men in fine dress mingle with artisans
and laborers, boatmen maneuver their crafts, a man and a dog
are pulled from the water. To the Venetian viewer such details
satisfied a taste for the accidental and the trivial. They made the
painted scene that much more credible because the ceremony of
consignment was, presumably, simply "caught" by the artist in the
confusion of life as it happens.

Many paintings in the Doge's Palace represented historical
events in purely allegorical terms. Jacopo Palma il Giovane painted
the *Allegory of the League of Cambrai* in the Senate Hall to commemorate one of the most perilous moments in Venetian history, when, moved by fear and resentment of Venice's imperial-
ism and ambition, the major European powers had formed an
alliance in 1508 to take over her subject cities in the Terraferma

(FIG. 49). After several humiliating military defeats, the worst of which was the Battle of Agnadello in the following year, Venice lost almost all her mainland possessions. Although Venetian armies regained the captured territories by 1517, the precariousness of the moment – with the very survival of the republic at risk – remained fresh in Venetian memories.

Palma visualizes the story in terms of a direct but elegantly choreographed confrontation. On the left Venetia, flanked by the civic virtues of Peace and Abundance and a combative Lion of St. Mark, brandishes a sword. Doge Leonardo Loredan is a still presence behind them, his arms extended in a gesture of supplication. Europa, astride a bull, attacks from the left, her shield bearing the arms of members of the League: the Emperor Maximilian, the pope, the King of France and the Duke of Milan. As the first city to return to the Venetian fold, Padua is visible in the background, thus signifying the positive outcome of the conflict.

Venice's eventual triumph is made clear by the winged victories who descend from the heavens holding palm fronds and a laurel wreath. It is important to note that they intend to crown the lion and not Doge Loredan. Although the living symbol of the state – and, as such, an intermediary with the divine – a Venetian doge was long on charisma and short on real power.

Primus inter pares

Indeed, it is important to distinguish between the office and the man. The dogeship was a quasi-sacral office, and doges represented something more than themselves as men. In the minds of the patriciate, their elected doge – for all the symbolic importance of his office – was but *primus inter pares* as a man: the first among equals, with the emphasis on the latter word. Accordingly, unlike many absolute monarchs of the time, the doge was hemmed in by a set of rules and obligations. These were set out in the ducal *promissione*, a document specially drawn up at the time of his election. Copies were made for the doge, the ducal chancery and the procurators. To ensure that the doge remained aware of his duties and of the limitations of his prerogatives, the law required that the text be read aloud to him every two months.

Official documents were often decorated with illuminations of considerable originality. A page in the *promissione* of Doge Antonio Grimani, who took office at the age of eighty-seven, shows the doge kneeling before St. Mark to be blessed as he receives from him the *vexillum* or standard of office (FIG. 50). The subject matter would have been familiar to any Venetian, for it had

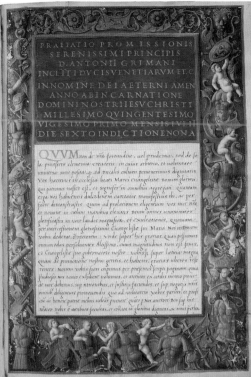

been a standard image on coins since the Middle Ages. But here
the illuminator has inserted it into a context of intriguing spa-
tial ambiguity with a clever play between nature and artifice. A
fanciful construction of acanthus scrolls, athletic *putti*, and zoomor-
phic structural elements creates a stage for the benediction ceremony and frames an aperture through which a convincing Terraferma landscape is visible. Clad in his ducal robes with an ermine
cape, the doge wears a linen cap, the *camauro*, on his head and has
not yet been crowned with the red velvet *corno* held by the
small boy behind him. The doge was given the courtesy title of
il Principe, and the *corno* was equivalent to a royal crown. Such
distinctions were symbolic dignities, but essential for the honor of
the republic in the world at large. They asserted the doge's supe-
riority to neighboring heads of state – and his equivalence to the
pope, the emperor and other crowned heads of Europe. Grimani,
who died less than two years after his coronation, called his
sons to his deathbed and asked them to preserve his copy of the
promissione "for the honor of our house."

Giovanni Bellini captured the hallowed majesty of the dogeship in a portrait of Leonardo Loredan painted shortly after he

50. *Promissione* of Doge
Antonio Grimani, 6 July
1521. Illumination on
vellum, 12 x 8¾" (30.5
x 22 cm). British Library,
London.

took office (FIG. 51). Using a familiar Venetian formula of the bust-length figure behind a ledge against a clear blue sky, he achieved an exquisite rendering of the exterior man and his dress. A sharp shadow models the thin aristocratic face, and now the *camauro* is covered with a white brocade *corno* that matches the doge's mantle. The sumptuous fabric is woven with a white-on-white pattern worked out in golden thread. The row of large buttons, called *campanoni d'oro* or golden bells, was also part of the ducal costume. Loredan was known for his fastidious dress, and Bellini gives him a dignified presence and even a certain warmth. And yet, for all his meticulous attention to detail, the artist nonetheless disjoins the doge from time and space. The man has become the office, and could as well be the reliquary bust of a saint sitting on a shelf with all the aura of a holy figure.

51. GIOVANNI BELLINI
Doge Leonardo Loredan,
c. 1501. Oil on panel, 24½
x 17¾" (61.6 x 45.1 cm).
National Gallery, London.

The doge's role as an intermediary between the Venetian people and the supernatural forces of heaven was given visual definition in the sequence of votive paintings in the Doge's Palace. Each doge was allowed to commission one upon his election. Sometimes these works came dangerously close to extolling the man more than the office, and the patriciate exercised constant vigilance to prevent the former from upstaging the latter. A surviving *modello* or sketch for Veronese's *Votive Painting of Doge Sebastiano Venier*, when compared to the finished work, shows a modification that may have been made in response to such concerns (FIGS 52 and 53). Elected in 1577/78, Venier ordered the painting to commemorate his heroic role as captain general of the Venetian navy in the Battle of Lepanto of 1571. The sea battle, visible in the background of the painting, was an emblematic event of the period and was much celebrated in public art and state propaganda.

After losing Cyprus to the Turks and seeing her maritime empire slipping away, Venice had joined with the pope and the King

of Spain in a Holy League to mount a new crusade. In a time of shifting alliances, it was not unusual for former enemies to become allies. The combined Christian forces numbered some forty to fifty thousand men manning 208 galleys, just over half of them commanded by Venetians. The Turkish fleet was of equal strength. When the two forces met in the Gulf of Patras near Lepanto, the Christians raised a crucifix on every galley and fought with crusading zeal. In an extremely bloody fight that was decided in hand-to-hand combat across the decks of all the galleys jammed

52. PAOLO VERONESE *Votive Painting of Doge Sebastiano Venier*, c. 1578. Oil on canvas, 9′3″ x 18′8½″ (2.8 x 5.7 m). Hall of the Collegio, Doge's Palace, Venice.

The Collegio was the steering committee of the Senate, the major locus of political power in Venice, and set the agenda for that body. The painting is installed directly above the tribunal where the doge sat with his councilors, a group called the Signoria.

53. PAOLO VERONESE *Modello* for the *Votive Painting of Doge Sebastiano Venier*, c. 1578. Oil sketch in chiaroscuro on prepared red paper, 11¾ x 18½″ (29.7 x 47 cm). British Museum, London.

together, the Christians lost nine thousand men and the Turks more than three times that number. In the end the victory was really only a symbolic one, for Venice never did regain Cyprus, her last important possession in the Aegean. But symbols are important, for if the Turks had won or the Christians had withdrawn without a fight, no Venetian ship could have sailed the Mediterranean for years to come without being at the mercy of the Turkish fleet.

In Veronese's preparatory drawing for Venier's painting, Venetia is the central focus of the scene. Crowned with a garland of roses, she displays the *corno* to the kneeling doge. His ducal mantle – identifiable as such by the *campanoni d'oro* on the shoulder – is swept back to reveal his battle armor, suggesting that his exploits at Lepanto had earned him the dogeship. To the left, the personification of Christian Faith raises a chalice, bringing it close to the ducal *corno*. St. Mark, accompanied by two figures, sits above her in the clouds and confers his benediction on the group below.

In the finished painting, Venetia, still holding the *corno*, is relegated to a less prominent position behind the doge. Taking her place front and center is a regal St. Giustina, on whose feast-day the battle had been won. Crowned with pearls, she is armed with a sword and the palm of victory. Christ is now brought in to dominate the scene, and St. Mark is transferred from the cloud to a supporting role behind Venier, where he takes his place next to another military hero.

While the drawing had privileged the mortal over the eternal, mystical doge, Veronese's changes give the painting a more universalizing character. By displacing Venetia and St. Mark, he made it less specific to the election of a particular doge. The Lion of St. Mark, however, maintained his pride of place in a central position in both versions. He was a more fluid sign, at once a heraldic animal and a symbol of the abstract concept of the state.

Symbols of State

Venice could be personified in human guise as Venetia, the Virgin, or even as Venus or other female figures, but the Lion of St. Mark – popularly called "our San Marco" – was the oldest and most universal symbol of the republic. Greeting visitors to the city from atop his column on the Piazzetta, he was also its ambassador abroad. In cities throughout the Terraferma and the *stato da mar*, he stood guard on top of columns and graced the city gates and facades of public palaces as a permanent reminder of Venetian dominion. He was also visible at close hand, and on a daily basis, on coins, banners, ducal seals, and official documents and proclamations, both inside and outside Venice.

It is important to remember that the Lion of St. Mark was a multi-valent image and more than just a sign of the republic and its presence. He was also a symbol of its divine destiny and ongoing protection. Carpaccio's *Lion of St. Mark* summed up the larger message (FIG. 54). Equipped with wings and a halo, the lion alludes to St. Mark's continuing protection of the city with one paw on an open book bearing an inscription: *PAX TIBI MARCE EVANGELISTA MEVS* (Peace unto you, Mark my evangelist).

According to a legend that dates back to the thirteenth century, these were the very words spoken by an angel to St. Mark himself in an episode called the *praedestinatio*. On this occasion, it was claimed, Mark had received a prophecy that his body would find its final resting place in Venice on the spot where the church of San Marco was to be built. Not only did the story justify Venice's pious theft and possession of the saint's relics, but it also served as proof of the city's holy predestination.

The lion's stance gives visual form to the fulfillment of that promise. With his front paws on the land and rear paws in the water, he symbolizes Venice's dominion over both land and sea. The political and religious center of the city and the source of its justice, piety, and tranquillity – the Doge's Palace, the Campanile, the domes of San Marco, the Torre dell'Orologio – is visible behind him along with the *bucintoro*, the ceremonial barge of the doge. To the right are the great galleys, the source of Venice's wealth and abundance, and the fortress of San Nicolò that guarded the sea entrance to the lagoon.

Justice, as the highest civic virtue, was another symbol of the republic, second in importance only to the Lion of St. Mark.

54. VITTORE CARPACCIO *Lion of St. Mark*, 1516. Canvas, 4'6¾" x 12'1" (1.4 x 3.7 m). Doge's Apartments (Sala delle Volte), Doge's Palace, Venice.

Painted in 1516 for the Magistracy of the Treasury, whose offices were located in the Palazzo dei Camerlenghi near the Rialto bridge, the work documents its own provenance, with the coats-of-arms of the five noble officials who commissioned it painted along the lower edge. Commissions of public art by office-holders were acceptable modes of self-aggrandizement in a patriciate of equals.

55. *Venecia-Justice*, mid-14th century. Stone relief. Piazzetta (west) facade of the Doge's Palace, Venice.

It made its first explicit appearance as an emblem of state in a sculpted roundel on the Piazzetta facade of the Doge's Palace above the seventh great column from the southwest corner (FIG. 55). Probably dating from the middle of the fourteenth century, the relief depicts a matron seated on a Solomonic throne of double lions. She holds a sword in her right hand and a scroll in the left bearing an inscription: *FORTIS / IUSTA / TRONO / FURIAS / MARE / SUB PEDE / PONO* (Just and strong, I am enthroned, I vanquish by sea the furies). The furies lying at her feet may be seen as the vices of Pride and Ire and – through an extension of the analogy – as the evils of civil discord and military threat. The female figure could be mistaken for a personification of Justice (and perhaps Fortitude) alone were it not for the inscription above her head – *VENECIA* – and the fact that she holds no scales.

In the early fifteenth century, two full-round sculptures of Justice were installed in even more prominent positions on the building: a standing figure that rises above the roofline and forms the pinnacle of the great balcony of the south facade facing the lagoon; and a seated figure atop the Porta della Carta, the main entrance to the palace complex. The association of the Doge's Palace with the virtues of justice and wisdom was underscored by a sculptural group of the *Judgement of Solomon* on the corner of the building erected to the right of the Porta della Carta in the 1420–30s to house offices involved in the administration of justice.

An even denser multi-layered elaboration of the theme was achieved in the decoration of three bronze flagpole bases cast by the sculptor Alessandro Leopardi and installed in front of the basilica of San Marco in 1505 (FIG. 56). Pietro Contarini, writing around 1541, described the central pedestal:

> The one in the middle shows three ships coming from the high seas. On the stern of the first ship one sees the golden Virgin of the Pole, who having been exiled by the wicked world, has fixed her abode in Venetian waters. In her right hand she has the honored sword, but in the left she holds the head of a convicted traitor. A merman guides her golden vessel; the prow bears the balanced scales.

56. ALESSANDRO LEOPARDI
Astraea-Justice, 1504.
Bronze pedestal in front of
the basilica of San Marco
on Piazza San Marco.

The Virgin of the Pole is to be identified as Astraea, the goddess of justice, introduced in Virgil's *Aeneid* as the harbinger of a new Golden Age. Two other vessels are included in the cortege that moves around the pedestal. They carry Ceres, "the Mother of the Granaries," who holds a leaf of wheat and a horn of fruit and represents Abundance, and "happy Victory in a white dress," who holds a palm branch in her right hand and spoils of the enemy in the left.

Astraea, holding a sword and vanquishing a figure of discord, is a graceful metamorphosis of the trecento relief of Venetia as Justice in the roundel on the west wall of the Palazzo Ducale into a conflation of Venetia-Justice-Astraea. But Francesco Sansovino, writing in 1581, made an even more expansive reading, suggesting that all three figures on the pedestal added up to a metaphor for the abstract idea of Venice as the sum of the civic virtues of Justice, Abundance, and Peace.

4 City Joyous and Triumphant

Exclaiming on a diplomatic visit in 1495 that Venice "is the most triumphant city that I have ever seen," the French ambassador Philippe de Commynes was particularly impressed by Venetian ceremonial. While every society had its recurring feasts, as well as ceremonies for special occasions, civic ritual in Venice was notable for its exceptional splendor. Spectacle, the most ephemeral of the visual arts, offered a unique opportunity to respond to the needs of a given moment while giving structure to the myth of Venice.

Overleaf
57. GENTILE BELLINI
Procession in the Piazza San Marco, 1496 (detail).
Canvas, whole work 12'
x 24' 5¼" (3.7 x 7.5 m).
Gallerie dell'Accademia,
Venice.

Gentile Bellini's *Procession in the Piazza San Marco* records an event held each year on 25 April, the feast-day of St. Mark (FIG. 57). Commissioned by the Scuola Grande di S. Giovanni Evangelista as part of a cycle of paintings that honored their miracle-working relic of the True Cross, the painting depicts members of the confraternity marching through the Piazza San Marco – the main ceremonial space of the city. Preceded by a choir and an honor guard of marchers holding huge candlesticks called *doppieri*, the relic is carried on a richly decorated platform under a canopy. The painting commemorates the miraculous healing of a child whose father, wearing a red toga, drops to his knees in supplication. He is just visible through a break in the procession to the right of the cross. The manner in which his personal act of devotion is embedded within the context of Venetian ceremonial life is characteristic of the eyewitness style of painting, of which Gentile was a leading exponent in the later years of the fifteenth century.

Significant in itself as a work of art, the painting also gives testimony to civic values. Although pride of place is given to the Scuola Grande di S. Giovanni Evangelista, the canopy is decorated with the coats-of-arms of all the *scuole grandi* of the city. The message is clear: all are included and consensus prevails. The bystanders scattered through the piazza, as well as the spectators who line the procession and fill the windows of palaces on the right-hand side, include young and old, religious and secular, male and female, foreign and local, rich and poor. In short, they mirror the diverse character of the Venetian polity.

The doge is visible at the far right, preceded by groups of standard-bearers and trumpeters and followed by patrician magistrates, with the highest-ranking officials marching closest to the doge. With the order of the procession determined by caste, office, and seniority, the procession gives visible definition to the Venetian constitution. Recurring and well orchestrated, such processions conveyed a reassuring message of order and stability. Indeed the special power of ritual lies in its repetition.

The coronation of a new doge was a ceremonial of a different sort. A happening outside the annual ritual agenda, it was surely inevitable, given the certain mortality of the doge, but it was not predictable. Although here, too, the ceremony was carefully planned according to rigid protocols, it belongs in the category of liminal moments: a time of transformation from one state of being to another.

When a law was passed in 1485 making the coronation of the doge a public event, construction was begun on a great ceremonial staircase in the courtyard of the Doge's Palace (FIG. 58).

Initiated by the architect Antonio Rizzo (active 1465; d. 1499/1500) during the term of Doge Marco Barbarigo, it was essentially completed around eight years later, during the dogeship of Barbarigo's brother Agostino. It came to be called the Scala dei Giganti after Jacopo Sansovino's colossal statues of Mars and Neptune were installed on the top landing in the mid-sixteenth century. The *scala* served as a monumental plinth for the doge, designed to frame and display him in spectacles of state. As Francesco Sansovino later put it: "From the Porta della Carta the staircase looks truly royal, [built] of the whitest marble [and] worked with trophies; standing at the base of the campanile one sees it from top to bottom . . ."

In the ducal coronation ceremony, the staircase was the culminating point of a lengthy ritual. The first phase began when the doge was presented to the citizenry from the porphyry pulpit in San Marco. He then moved to the high altar, where he was invested with the *vexillum* of St. Mark – the mystical source of ducal authority – in a reenactment of the ritual depicted in Antonio Grimani's *promissione* (see FIG. 50, page 77). The second phase took place in Piazza San Marco, where the doge was carried on a platform by sailors from the Arsenal and made a symbolic display of ducal largess by tossing coins into the crowd.

59. JOST AMMAN
The Feast of the Sensa,
c. 1560 (detail). Woodcut
with watercolor, whole
work 21¼″ x 8′5¾″ (54 cm
x 2.6 m). Graphische
Sammlung der Staatsgalerie,
Stuttgart.

Finally, he was carried through the Porta della Carta into a shaded passageway toward the shining staircase. After ascending it on foot between a double row of his electors, he reached the top landing and took the oath of office. Swearing to abide by the provisions of the ducal *promissione*, he was crowned with the *camauro* and a costly jeweled *corno*, called the *zoia* – the symbol of supreme political authority. While the ritual clearly posited the source of ducal prerogatives in the patriciate through its electors, once the power was handed over to the doge during his coronation, the top landing of the staircase was transformed from a place of ritual to a place of rule.

Pageantry and civic ritual refreshed the force of political symbols through repeated exposure in public space. The *trionfi*, as the insignia purportedly granted the doge by Pope Alexander III in 1177, were essential components of the ducal procession. They accompanied the doge on those dignified excursions into civic space referred to by the phrase *andar in trionfo* (to go in triumph).

The Feast of the Sensa was depicted in a woodcut by the Flemish artist Jost Amman, probably after a lost original by Titian

The Splendor of Holiness

69. View of the Sala
Grande of the Scuola Grande
di S. Rocco, Venice.

Six decades later, in 1581, Francesco Sansovino saw the painting as
the basis of the Scuola Grande di S. Rocco's prosperity:

> They made, therefore, the facade of their fraternity all incrusted
> with the most noble marbles and rich with ornaments, at incred-
> ible expense. In which enterprise [they were] helped greatly
> by an image of Christ painted many years ago by Titian; mak-
> ing diverse miracles, it was patronized with the most ample
> alms and gifts, not just from all of Venice, but also the sur-
> rounding cities. Then having grown through calamitous times
> of plague (which has often brought trouble to these parts)
> by means of alms, bequests, and other profits and benefits, [San
> Rocco] finally became the richest confraternity of all.

By Sansovino's time, Jacopo Tintoretto had completed the sumptuous decoration of the *piano nobile* of the Scuola Grande di S.
Rocco with scenes from the Old and New Testaments. They lined
the walls and were inserted in heavy gilded compartments on
the ceilings (FIG. 69). After painting the first canvas free of charge,
Tintoretto joined the *scuola* and promised to devote the rest of his

life to the pictorial embellishment of its meeting house. Delivering three paintings a year on the feast day of St. Roch, he went on to decorate the walls of the ground floor in a campaign that eventually included sixty canvases. The building as a whole can be considered one of the greatest decorative achievements of the entire Renaissance period.

The values implied in Sansovino's statement sit uneasily with the pious and charitable concerns of the *scuole grandi*. Citing the *scuole grandi* as "the best things that Venice has," the Milanese ambassador had written in 1497:

> their revenues are spent in part on decorating the scuole, all of which have elaborate and gilded ceilings, and are now becoming more imposing than ever: their buildings are being embellished with facades of marble and stone of great value. Some of the revenues are spent on the many religious services that they perform continuously, where they dispense innumerable candles; and the balance is spent on helping members of each scuola . . . There are always many infirm among them, who are cared for, fed and clothed, along with their families, until they get well or die.

At issue was the proper way to honor the holy. The impulse to build was sanctioned by the long-standing view that architectural splendor, costly decorations, and elaborate ceremony were considered just as essential for the proper expression of religious devotion as charity and the care of the poor.

Ecclesiastical splendor also had a political dimension. Magnificent churches and lavish meeting houses for the *scuole* were important for the honor – and protection – of the state. The church of S. Maria dei Miracoli is an exquisite example of civic holiness (FIG. 70). Built as a votive chapel to house a particular miracle-working image of the Madonna that was once framed in a *capitello* on a street corner, it was completely financed by public donations. Pietro Lombardo, its architect, was literally given *carte blanche*. Ordered to seek out the finest Greek, Carrara and Veronese marbles, *verde antico* (polished green serpentine or marble) and porphyry, he covered all the wall surfaces, both inside and out. The interior of the raised choir, crowned by a dome, features sumptuous and innovative *all'antica* carving of marble sea creatures by Pietro's son, Tullio Lombardo, and creates a special stage for the miracle-working image on the high altar. The barrel vault above the nave with its elaborate gilded compartments, each containing the bust-length painting of an Old Testament prophet,

was constructed *alla veneziana* – in the Venetian manner. The building has often been justifiably likened to a precious jewel box or reliquary chest – a most appropriate container for the venerated icon that it was built to honor and to protect.

70. View of the nave of S. Maria dei Miracoli, Venice.

71. PAOLO VERONESE
Marriage Feast at Cana,
1562–63. Oil on canvas,
21'11½" x 32'5¾" (6.7
x 9.9 m). Louvre, Paris.

Among the hundred or so
guests is a group of
Venetian painters posing as
musicians in the central
foreground. Identifiable
from other portraits are
Veronese, dressed in white,
and Tintoretto behind him
to the right, both playing
the *viola da braccio*. Titian,
dressed in red, sits on the
right side of the table,
playing the *viola da gamba*.
Between them the figure
playing the flute has been
associated with Jacopo
Bassano, but the younger
man playing an early
version of the violin is
unidentified.

Simple stories could also be set by painters in splendid settings. The Benedictine monastery of S. Giorgio Maggiore was one of the richest in Venice when Paolo Veronese was commissioned to decorate the end wall of its refectory. The monks of S. Giorgio would have been aware of the artist's huge pageant-like scenes of historical, allegorical, and biblical subjects and were thus opting for a splendid display. Indeed, although refectories, as monastic dining rooms, typically featured paintings of the Last Supper, Veronese and his patrons responded to the Venetian taste for spectacle and chose the altogether more festive theme of the *Marriage Feast at Cana* (FIG. 71). Like many of Veronese's works, the painting has a theatrical quality. The architecture is of a noble classical style, with a Doric order in the foreground and a Corinthian order behind. But although the composition seems to promise a view into deep space, it is effectively closed off by the balustrade that cuts across the canvas and defines a stage in the foreground that is packed with wedding guests. In a densely articulated narrative mode, analogous to the eyewitness style of about fifty years earlier, here too the main event is embedded in a profusion of seemingly trivial detail. In fact, nineteenth (and even twentieth) century critics called the *Marriage Feast at Cana* indecorous, complaining that it had too many figures and too many distractions. Indeed, they argued, the religious message simply got swallowed up in all that opulence and splendor.

But this kind of criticism misses the point. Although the bride and groom are relegated to an inconspicuous location on the far left, Christ, whose miraculous transformation of water into wine is being celebrated in the painting, is placed in the center, just like in Leonardo's *Last Supper*. Here again, he is both the quiet observer and the effective agent of the miracle.

Directly in front of Christ on a table surrounded by a group of musicians is an hourglass. It symbolizes music as measured time and suggests that the hour has come. On the balcony behind Christ, butchers are cutting up meat with cleavers. Taken together, the two contrasting activities define the central axis and probably allude to Christ's coming sacrifice.

One of the notable features of this work is the great mixture of costumes: Turkish, contemporary Venetian, antique. Expanders of time and of space, they broaden the geographical and chronological context of the event and help to draw the scene right into the present. So opulence has a purpose here. To Venetian eyes it would not have trivialized a religious mystery. Rather it ennobled it and imbued it with a meaning that was both timeless and also specific to the times.

The Face of Poverty

During the Counter-Reformation period, the debate on splendor versus charity had heightened, and many of the *scuole* were sharply criticized for their luxurious tastes. Aside from the growing gap between rich and poor with ever greater disparities of wealth, class lines had become more firmly drawn. Emphasizing assistance to the deserving poor and punishment of the able-bodied who chose to "practice the trades of the beggar and the cheat," the Venetian Senate passed a comprehensive poor law in 1529:

> Charity is, without any doubt, to be considered the most important form of good work, and it must always be practiced towards our neighbors. As is everyone's duty, we must look to the interests of the poor and the health of the sick and offer food to the hungry; and never should we fail to extend our aid and favour to those who can earn their bread by the sweat of their brow.

72. TINTORETTO
Annunciation, 1583–87.
Oil on canvas, 13'10" x 17'10½" (4.2 x 5.5 m).
Scuola Grande di S. Rocco, Venice.

The debate is reflected in the visual arts, but not always in a straightforward manner. In many of his New Testament scenes for the

73. Jacopo Bassano
Lazarus and the Rich Man,
c. 1554. Oil on canvas,
4′9″¹/₂ x 7′4″ (1.46 x 2.23 m).
The Cleveland Museum of Art.

Scuola Grande di S. Rocco, Tintoretto displayed a pronounced ambivalence. In the *Annunciation*, Mary sits in a room furnished with an elegant canopied bed and a gilded compartmented ceiling (FIG. 72). Its wall is dilapidated, nonetheless, with brick masonry that is awkwardly patched with mortar augmenting part of a classical column base. Inside the room, a fraying straw-bottomed chair shows unmistakable signs of age. At once splendid and humble, the setting recalls Christ's modest origins, suggests the passage of time, and documents the end of classical civilization.

A disjunction of a different sort is seen in Jacopo Bassano's (c. 1515–92) *Lazarus and the Rich Man* (FIG. 73). Here the artist depicts a parable from the Gospel of St. Luke (16:19–31), often cited by preachers to make the point that the poor will receive their reward in heaven, while the rich will pay dearly for their wealth. Dives, the rich man, dressed in fine clothes and feasted magnificently every day, while a poor leper named Lazarus lay starving – and ignored – at his gate. Dogs would come and lick the man's sores. When he died, angels carried him directly into Abraham's embrace in heaven. Dives, by contrast, was consigned to the eternal torments of Hades.

In Bassano's painting, the scene is set in an elegant loggia constructed with heavy classical columns. Dives sits at a table covered with an oriental carpet and a fine linen cloth and holds a golden plate in his hand. He is joined by a musician and a beautiful woman – probably a courtesan – who is dressed in a low-cut gown of red velvet that reveals a generous expanse of snowy white skin. Lazarus, clad in rags, lies on the ground hoping for crumbs. Literally unseen by the convivial group at the table and ignored even by a young servant boy in the foreground, he is acknowledged only by the dogs.

What was the purpose of works such as this? They were surely commissioned by the rich to hang in their homes as a permanent reminder of their obligations to the poor. But there is a tension here between the moralizing message and the manner in which it is depicted. The luxurious lifestyle is presented in an unambiguously attractive manner. The poor beggar is simply one more trapping of that lifestyle, emphasizing it by contrast, but in an unthreatening way. Most significantly, any reference to Dives's unfortunate destiny is excluded altogether. Such a painting offers a means to avoid dealing directly with a social problem by "aestheticizing" it and incorporating it unproblematically within a world of leisure and privilege. Art could thus serve once more as a mediating factor, helping to bridge the gap between religious values and secular aspirations.

The Lure of the Antique

By subsuming artifacts and reminiscences of the pagan world into Christian imagery, art also reflected changing attitudes toward the ancient past. Venetian painters of the fifteenth century participated in the revival of antiquity with responses that ranged from the romantic to the archaeological. A painter from one of Venice's Aegean possessions, Fra Antonio Falier da Negroponte (active 1450–60s), encountered the classicizing inventions of Jacopo Bellini, Mantegna, and Donatello with a particularly receptive eye and open mind. He worked for a time in Venice, where he produced only one work that can be attributed to him with any certainty: an altarpiece notable for its uncritical embrace of the imagery of the ancient world (FIG. 60, page 91).

Fra Antonio, though a Franciscan friar, had a fine eye for fashion, clothing the Madonna in a cloak of costly Venetian brocade trimmed with pearls. She is seated on an elaborate throne in a paradise garden, abundant with fruit trees, small birds, and flowering shrubs. While the environment of flora and fauna can be associated with the traditional International-style iconography of Gentile da Fabriano and Pisanello (c. 1395–1445/6), the scene is enriched with new citations of a fanciful antiquarian character.

The throne, though Gothic in conception, is decorated with exuberantly classicizing, but patently unclassical, reliefs of portrait busts, cornucopiae, *bucrania* (ox skulls), playful *putti,* and Hellenistic looking figures wearing filmy garments *all'antica* (in the antique style). The central lobe of the throne base is adorned with the *tricipitium* – a grouping of three heads that appeared in a number of architectural settings in Venice as a late antique symbol of prudence (see also FIG. 36, page 57). Presumably untroubled by the theological implications of his wholesale appropriation of pagan imagery for Christian purposes, Fra Antonio may well have been influenced by the architectural fantasies of Jacopo Bellini. He too did not hesitate to apply a classical decorative vocabulary to Gothic buildings. It is also important to remember that although Renaissance humanism was concerned with pagan accomplishments, it

74. CIMA DA CONEGLIANO *Madonna and Child with SS. Michael and Andrew,* c. 1496–98. Panel, 6′4¹/₂″ x 4′4³/₄″ (1.9 x 1.3 m). Galleria Nazionale, Parma.

was not anti-religious. The aim was to augment, and not to replace, Christian teachings with the inspired wisdom of the ancient world – a syncretic approach that extended into art as well.

Cima da Conegliano, a painter from a Veneto town north of Venice that was part of the Venetian Terraferma and cultural milieu, represented the next generation of gifted immigrants. He approached the classical world with a greater sense of decorum. In an altarpiece in Parma, he places the Madonna on the crumbling doorstep of a ruinous classical building (FIG. 74). Once splendidly adorned with pilasters carved with *grotteschi*, a marble revetment, and monumental columns, it is counterbalanced by the view of a hill town, identifiable as the *castello* of Conegliano. The landscape was thus relevant to the artist and not to its original placement in the Franciscan Observant church of SS. Annunziata in Parma. Saints Michael and Andrew, however, would have been specific to the patron as intercessors both spiritual and visual between the worshipper and the Virgin and Child.

The asymmetrical scheme, later to become a distinctively Venetian format for altarpieces, was still a novelty at the time. Her lower body positioned toward the left and her torso twisted and tilted to the right, the Virgin is the focus and facilitator of the composition – the link between the architecture in the foreground and the deep landscape vista behind. Unlike Fra Antonio's ingenuous pastiche, Cima's painting preaches a moralizing sermon. The pagan ruins mark the end of the old order; the Madonna and Child, with the saints and the hill town, signal the advent of the new. The crystalline atmosphere, meticulous detail, and fine finish make the work a culminating statement of quattrocento empiricism.

With Sebastiano del Piombo's (c. 1485–1547) *Judgement of Solomon*, the Venetian viewer was brought into a living classical world (FIG. 75). Unlike Fra Antonio or even Cima, Sebastiano reveals a new archaeological exactitude and a sense of historical consistency. Appropriately, the setting for the scene of judgement is a basilica, the ancient site of Roman justice. The double-aisled, arcaded interior, with a golden half-dome above the throne, is constructed with the Corinthian order of architecture in a late antique style. Sebastiano turns the centralized composition of the *sacra conversazione* – the holy figure flanked by saints – to narrative purposes and achieves Albertian rationalism, dynamism, and a rigorous clarity. But although the perspectival system was care-

75. SEBASTIANO DEL PIOMBO *Judgement of Solomon*, begun c. 1508–09. Canvas, 6'10" x 10'4" (2.1 x 3.2 m). The National Trust, Kingston Lacy, Dorset.

Infra-red photographs reveal two earlier versions of the composition, one with a horseman. Venetian painters in this period frequently worked out their compositions on the canvas itself, in contrast to Florentine practice which called for a well-formulated preparatory design.

fully planned, with the receding and lateral lines of the pavement incised in the gesso (white gypsum) ground, the work was never completed: the babies are missing, the executioner lacks his sword, and passages throughout the work still reveal their underpainting. And yet the story is told through the gestures. Even though something is clearly missing, the viewer has no problem in imagining the as yet unpainted children. The raised arm of the executioner, about to deliver a sword blow, implies the body of a living child beneath it. The true mother, standing behind him, holds her hand to her heart in artless sincerity. With her head tilted to one side and a facial expression bespeaking tenderness and a lack of guile, she represents a new canon of female beauty that appeared in Venetian art in this period: ample curves, soft skin, and a gentle sensuality. The false mother, by contrast, bends forward in an awkward pose that has the forced, insistent quality of one who does not have the reassurance of truth on her side. With her back to the viewer and her shadowed face visible only in partial profile, she appears to be less than candid as she points to the spot where her dead baby would have been painted.

The protagonists are not wholly of the ancient world, for the two mothers and the youth on the right are all clothed in modern Venetian dress. And yet, such is the structural coherence of the scene that one is not aware of the temporal disjunction. Sebastiano moved permanently to Rome in 1511 – probably the reason for the unfinished state of the painting – but already his work has a quality of *romanitas*, with an underlying geometry, weighty figures and a grand rhetorical style.

76. GIOVANNI BELLINI
Madonna of the Little Trees, 1487. Panel,
29 x 22³/₄″ (74 x 58 cm).
Gallerie dell'Accademia,
Venice.

Nature and Transcendence

The natural world, particularly the verdant landscapes that were so poignantly absent from lagoon life, was another special concern of Venetian painters. Already in the thirteenth century, Franciscan teachings were making people aware of the spiritual qualities of nature. Such views were brought to artistic fruition in the paintings of Giovanni Bellini. Even in his small devotional paintings, such as the *Madonna of the Little Trees*, the landscape background is more than just a setting (FIG. 76). The two small trees that flank the Virgin are prominent enough to suggest a symbolic meaning – perhaps standing for the Old and New Testaments. Behind them the peaks of the lower Alps dissolve in the haze of the afternoon sun. The same light falls on the Virgin and Christ, placing them in the world of the beholder. And yet, Bellini creates for them a privileged space within that world through the use of a favorite formula: the parapet that links and separates that space from our own; and the cloth of honor that demarcates it from the background. But there are counter-tendencies that provide a delicate balance between distance and approach. For example, the cloth hanging, of green moiré bordered in red, creates a chromatic bridge between the Madonna's gown and

77. LORENZO LOTTO *St. Jerome in the Wilderness*, 1506. Oil on panel, 19 x 15¼" (48 x 40 cm). Louvre, Paris.

the fields that stretch out behind her. Furthermore, while the mother's attention is focused on her child, he looks out at the viewer from the protective embrace of her hands. By bringing the holy figures down to earth, Bellini imbues the natural surroundings with an aura of the sacred.

Bellini's landscape remains essentially a separate realm; while the viewer is involved in it visually, the painted figures are not really part of it physically. Inevitably, Bellini sought ways to create a rational painted landscape into which the human figure is convincingly integrated. His painting of St. Francis in the Frick Collection in New York was a forerunner of a long line of pastoral paintings of religious themes, such as Lorenzo Lotto's *St. Jerome in the Wilderness* (FIG. 77). Here, the saint is an important presence in the scene, but his participation is of a quiet, retiring sort. Surrounded by huge boulders and wooded crags, he is embraced by a wilderness that is no longer simply a backdrop. Rather, it has an independent reality of its own. As Jerome averts his gaze from the beholder and withdraws into that reality, his left arm – indeed, his body – forms a diagonal that almost parallels the rock formation behind him, and his drapery plays against the edge of the outcropping on which he rests.

78. Tintoretto
*St. Mary of Egypt in
Meditation*, 1583–87.
Oil on canvas, 13'11$\frac{1}{3}$"
x 6'11" (4.3 x 2.1 m).
Pianterreno, Scuola di S.
Rocco, Venice.

The painting is located at
the end of the right-hand
wall of the hall, opposite a
pendant painting of Mary
Magdalene. Also a reformed
prostitute and a model of
the penitent sinner, Mary of
Egypt experienced a sudden
conversion on a visit to
Jerusalem. She retired to the
desert beyond the River
Jordan with three loaves of
bread and lived there alone
for many years in penitence
and prayer.

81. JOHN RUSKIN
Ca' da Mosto, 1852. Pencil and watercolor, 13½ x 19″ (34 x 48.2 cm). Birmingham City Museum and Art Gallery.

Ruskin wrote *The Stones of Venice* (1851–53) in praise of Venetian Gothic architecture. Deploring the neglect and ruinous condition of the earlier buildings, he made numerous sketches and wash drawings to record them for posterity. He annotated this drawing: "Two beautiful birds and an animal eating another, Broken and stained plaster."

ranging from the purely ornamental – plant motifs, birds, animals – to the quasi-magical. The latter category included positive symbols such as Hercules and icons of Christ, as well as metaphors of virtue triumphing over evil – for example, an eagle killing a hare or a snake. But there were also negative signs: demons, fighting animals, centaurs, and sirens. Such images probably had an apotropaic function: if symbols of evil, they could ward off enemies and prevent misfortune from entering the house; if symbols of good, they could protect the family within. No longer in fashion in the sixteenth century, *patere* and *formelle* still formed part of the palimpsest of the urban fabric. Some remaining in place and others migrating to walls of churches or interior courtyards, they retained their symbolic power, with new readings given in response to current circumstance. In 1509, Doge Leonardo Loredan thus interpreted three such plaques as political metaphors and cited

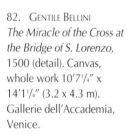

82. GENTILE BELLINI
The Miracle of the Cross at the Bridge of S. Lorenzo, 1500 (detail). Canvas, whole work 10'7¼" x 14'1¼" (3.2 x 4.3 m). Gallerie dell'Accademia, Venice.

The painting documents an episode in which the reliquary of the True Cross owned by the Scuola Grande di S. Giovanni Evangelista fell from the bridge and hovered miraculously above the water until Andrea Vendramin, the Guardian Grande, retrieved it. Frescoed facades are visible at the left.

a carving of a weeping woman, "who is interpreted by many as Venice" as a warning against going to war with the emperor.

Frescoes would eventually replace the small sculpted reliefs as the facade adornment of choice. In 1495 on a trip along the Grand Canal, the French ambassador Philippe de Commynes observed: "The palaces are very large and tall, and of good stone, and the old ones are all painted." Indeed, by his time, Venice was becoming an *urbs picta* – a painted city (FIG. 82). The earliest such decoration highlighted parts of buildings with feigned masonry or festoons, tapestries and carpets, but figurative motifs and grotesques of an antique character – vegetal, animal and human – became increasingly popular over time. Unlike facade paintings in Florence and Rome which tended to be in monochrome grisaille, the Venetian frescoes were typically painted with a many-hued palette of colors. Sixty-eight painted facades are recorded in early written sources. Seven of them attributable to Giorgione, they were decorated with such mythological figures as Bacchus, Venus, Mars, and Mercury, as well as poets, musicians, and female nudes. However, as Vasari later observed, the frescoes began to deteriorate in the damp Venetian climate as soon as they were painted. Today, only faded fragments remain of Venice's early multicolored face.

Domestic Space

Behind those resplendent facades lay the more private world of domestic space. The main entrance to a palace faced the waterway and served both the *fondaco* or commercial business on the *pianterreno* (ground floor) and the *piano nobile* and upper floors where the wealthy family lived. The basic floor plan, a tripartite scheme that originally derived from Byzantine models, was already well-established in the thirteenth century and survived with variants until the end of the republic (FIG. 83). Its most prominent feature is a large central hall called a *portego* that runs from front to back. Sometimes taking an *L* or a *T* shape when combined with an open gallery or loggia running across the front, this was the heart of the house and served as the main living and entertaining area. In patrician homes, it typically held a display of family trophies and weapons called a *lanziera di arme*, which could include animal skulls from the hunt and such spoils of battle as banners, armor, spears, swords, and scimitars. Significantly, all these signs of high birth and aristocratic distinction were located above ground-floor storerooms filled with merchandise from the family business – sacks of sugar, bales of wool, or maybe boxes of spices.

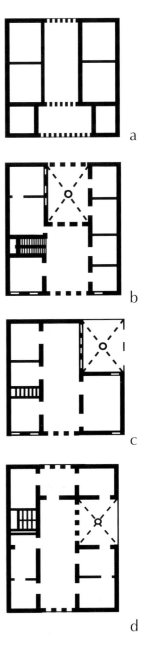

83. Variations of the traditional Venetian *casa-fondaco*.
a) Byzantine tripartite plan;
b) *U*-shaped plan;
c) *L*-shaped plan;
d) *C*-shaped plan.

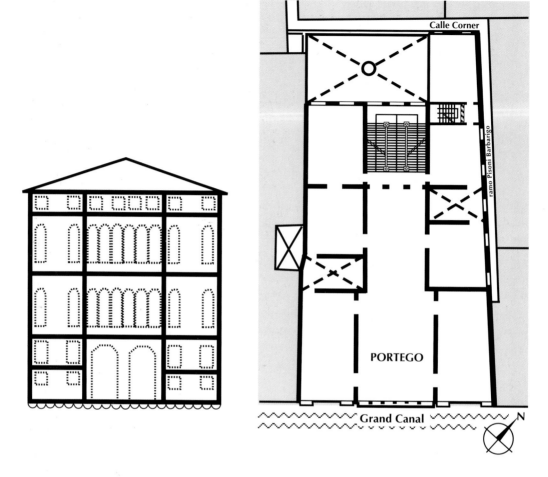

84. Palazzo Pisani-Moretta. Front elevation and plan of the lower *piano nobile*. Constructed in the mid-15th century, the palace features an evolved version of the traditional tripartite plan and was probably intended to house two families. It incorporates two courtyards at the sides, making a double *C* plan, as well as a larger courtyard in the rear, a feature of an *L* plan.

The *portego* was flanked by smaller rooms at the sides where the kitchen and the bedrooms were located. The tripartite plan was efficient in terms of making use of every bit of available space, but it often provided little light into the interior rooms and adaptations were called for. The primary innovation was the incorporation of a walled courtyard to give more light and air to the central block (FIG. 84). This open space could be moved around, depending on the site, and produced plans with *L*, *C* or *U* shapes. Although most ground-plans were quite irregular in shape because of the watery origins of Venetian building sites, the symmetrical Byzantine facades characteristic of many of the earliest buildings remained popular throughout the fifteenth century, standing alongside such Gothic palaces as the Ca' d'Oro whose facades were organized with a carefully calculated asymmetry.

Moving inside the Venetian palace, the significant decorative role played by light becomes apparent: not only the natural sun-

light and moonlight that streamed in through the great screen of windows on the facades, both front and rear, but also the artificial light from lamps and candles, as well as reflections of every kind on glass, mirrors, bronzes, and shining terrazzo floors (FIG. 85). The terrazzo floor is a glassy-smooth surface, made of colored cement with chips of stone embedded in it. And just as the exteriors of the palaces are like stage sets, the interiors function in the same way as box seats in a theater, for the windows are made for looking out of as well as for drawing in the light. This makes for a very different relationship between public and private

85. The Salone del Guarana, on the piano nobile of the Palazzo Pisani-Moretta.

The room is named after its ceiling fresco by Jacopo Guarana (1720–1808).

space than can be found in most other cities of the period, where houses were like fortresses, and windows were small and often fitted with oiled paper or cloth rather than with translucent glass.

The domestic interior, by virtue of its private character and the portability of furnishings, is more difficult to reconstruct than the halls of church and state. Much has perished, much has been redecorated, much has been sold off. In order to recapture an image of such rooms as they would have appeared in the Renaissance, it is first necessary to imagine them without the decorative accretions of later periods. Then with the help of inventories, early descriptions, and the handful of Venetian paintings that depict interiors, one may get a sense of the decorating conventions of the time. Finally, the reconstituted spaces must be restocked mentally with numerous objects – furniture and wall decoration, paintings, bronze and marble sculptures, glassware, ceramics, and the like – that have long been detached from their original settings.

The Art of Living

In 1494, Fra Pietro Casola, a Milanese priest of noble background, toured Venice in the company of the Milanese ambassador. Although their itinerary focused on churches and other public buildings, they also visited a private palace to pay their respects to a patrician lady in childbed, the wife of a member of the noble Dolfin family. The visit had been specially arranged, Casola suspected, "to show the splendor and great magnificence of the Venetian gentlemen." The comment is revealing. Although the home was to a large degree the extent of a woman's world – aside from the parish church – it still defined the husband's status. As Sabba da Castiglione (1485–1554) would later write in his *Ricordi*, a book of moral reflections published in Venice in 1546, "great gentlemen, rich, ingenious and magnificent . . . delight very much in adorning and furnishing their palaces, their houses, and especially the chambers and the studies with various and diverse ornaments, according to the variety and diversity of their ingenuity and fantasy . . ."

When asked his opinion about what he saw, Casola wrote: "I could only reply with a shrug of the shoulders, for it was estimated that the ornamentation of the room . . . had cost 2,000 ducats and more." The room that Casola saw is gone forever, but Giovanni Mansueti's painting of an interior in the palace of a certain Ser Nicolò Benvegnudo who lived in the *sestiere* of S. Polo (one of the six administrative units of the city) is remarkably close to his description (FIG. 86):

The fireplace was all of Carrara marble, shining like gold, and carved so subtly with figures and foliage that Praxitiles and Phidias could do no better. The ceiling was so richly decorated with gold and ultramarine and the walls so well adorned, that my pen is not equal to describing them. The bedstead alone was valued at five hundred ducats, and it was fixed in the room in the Venetian fashion. There were so many beautiful and natural figures and so much gold everywhere that I do not know whether in the time of Solomon . . . in which silver was reputed more common than stones, there was such abundance as was displayed there.

Ser Nicolò's room, with its carved fireplace, an abundance of gold, and a coffered ceiling painted with gilt and ultramarine, measures up well to Casola's observations. Though sparsely furnished, it has

86. GIOVANNI MANSUETI *Miraculous Healing of the Daughter of Ser Nicolò Benvegnudo of S. Polo,* c. 1502–06 (detail). Canvas, whole work 11′9¹/₄″ x 9′8¹/₂″ (3.6 x 3 m). Gallerie dell'Accademia, Venice.

The work belonged to the cycle of the Miracles of the True Cross painted for the Scuola Grande di San Giovanni Evangelista.

87. Velvet cloth of gold, woven in Venice at the end of the 15th century. Fragment, 32³/₄ x 21¹/₂″ (83 x 54.5 cm). Museo Civico Correr, Venice.

The background is yellow silk taffeta woven with a gold brocade weft forming loops that catch the light and create a sparkling effect (*allucciolatura*). The pattern, defined by velvet pile of red silk cut in two heights, includes a mandorla and pomegranate flowers surrounded by vegetal motifs of acanthus leaves and palmettes.

patterned curtains in the doorways, an elaborate gilded child's crib instead of a built-in bed, and a *lettuccio* on the right-hand wall. This was a wooden bench with an upholstered backrest made of a luxury fabric, probably silk, with the coats of arms of husband and wife embroidered or woven into the design. These insignia of family identity were used on many domestic objects. In fact, another is carved in relief on the mantlepiece.

Ser Nicolò's *lettuccio* offers but a tantalizing glimpse of the textiles that made Venetian cloth manufacturing famous throughout Europe (FIG. 87). A sumptuary law passed in 1476 allowed the use of taffeta for wall hangings and other furnishings in Venetian homes, but forbade more luxurious stuffs: cloth of gold or silver, velvet, brocade, and satin. Politically motivated to ensure the equality of the patriciate and to pacify religious reformers, such laws were generally ignored by wealthy gentlemen, who were more than willing to pay a fine to furnish their houses with the richest materials.

The art of silk-making in Venice had reached a high level of technical perfection in the fourteenth century with the immigration of exiles from Lucca who were highly skilled in spinning and weaving. The quality was carefully controlled. With raw silk imported from Syria, Turkey, and Persia, two thousand looms were in operation by the end of the fifteenth century, producing velvets, brocades, and silk damask both for domestic use and for export.

Seemingly, few objects in a prosperous Renaissance home escaped embellishment. Architectural elements such as banisters, pilasters, and ceiling beams were decorated with intaglio inlays or with painted designs, as in Ser Nicolò's chamber, and fabrics were worked with embroidery or trimmed with lace. Many fabrics were embroidered in professional workshops, but embroidery – both a craft and a cultivated pursuit – was also considered a suitable activity for high-born women. One of the earliest printed books of embroidery designs was published in Venice in 1527 by Giovanni Antonio Tagliente. A similar handbook announced that it aimed "to teach delightful young ladies how to embroider." Lacemaking was also women's work. Although Venetian women were skilled at needlepoint lace, Venice was particularly renowned for its bobbin lace (FIGS 88 and 89).

88. Bobbin lace-making pillow. Venice, 16th–17th century. Wood and stuffed hemp. Musei Civici, Centro Studi di Storia del Tessuto e del Costume, Venice.

According to a long-standing, and probably erroneous, tradition, the bobbin lace technique had developed from the making of fishing nets. Using linen thread wound around a bobbin, the pattern is worked out around an arrangement of pins stuck in a "pillow."

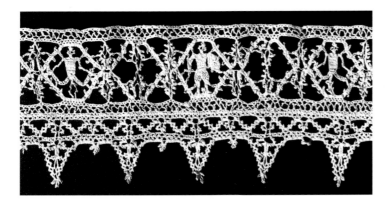

89. *Merletti* (bobbin lace) border, second half of the 16th century. Linen, 5¹⁄₂" x 7'6" (14 cm x 2.3 m). Museo Civico Correr, Venice.

The term *merletti* – "little battlements," – refers to the "points" of the border that resemble crenellations running along the roofline of a building. The border contains figural elements framed by hexagons.

Carpaccio decorated the bedchamber of St. Ursula in a more subdued manner than that of Ser Nicolò's, with less gold and no fireplace visible (FIG. 79, page 117), but the room is dominated by a canopied bed suitable for a princess, with coats of arms – those sure signs of aristocratic status – on its headboard and on the lintel of the doorway to the rear. The framed painting of the Madonna and Child illuminated by a votive lamp on the left-hand wall, featured in the same position in Ser Nicolò's room, was an element drawn from life. Inventories indicate that ninety percent of artisan homes contained at least one painting; the upper classes would have had more. While there were many paintings of saints, the Madonna, called *Nostra Donna*, was by far the most popular subject; she was the protectress of the house. Many such paintings were Byzantine icons, images which were thought to be endowed with a particular holiness. Described in inventories as *alla greca*, hundreds of icons were imported into Venice from Crete to be sold there in the city and elsewhere in the west. The demand was so great that replicas were also made in Venice by a cadre of local artists of modest artistic talent, who were

90. TITIAN
Gypsy Madonna, c. 1512.
Oil on panel, 26 x 33" (65.8 x 83.5 cm).
Kunsthistorisches Museum, Vienna.

called *madonneri*. Venetian artists also produced numerous works that were painted without gold-leaf backgrounds in a more naturalistic Renaissance style. Giovanni Bellini's workshop was particularly active in this regard, providing small devotional paintings of the Madonna and Child, often set within the Terraferma landscape so beloved to Venetian patrons (see FIG. 76; page 112). Titian continued the tradition with his *Gypsy Madonna* (FIG. 90). Featuring a red and green color scheme, it also would have harmonized with the interior decoration, for the inventories reveal that these were the most popular colors in the middle-class home.

A Woman's World

The red and green color scheme reappears in yet another painting by Carpaccio, whose *Birth of the Virgin* broadens our vision of the domestic environment to embrace the home of the prosperous artisan, complete with kitchen (FIG. 91). As in Ursula's bedchamber, a rich green fabric, now bordered with a delicate tracery of gold embroidery, hangs on the wall as a decorative form of insulation in a damp, and often icy climate. St. Anne reclines in a built-in bed, probably the type that Casola had referred to as

91. VITTORE CARPACCIO
Birth of the Virgin, 1504–08. Oil on canvas, 49$\frac{1}{2}$ x 50$\frac{3}{4}$" (1.3 x 1.3 m). Accademia Carrara, Bergamo.

The work was part of a cycle of five paintings of the Life of the Virgin painted for the Scuola di S. Maria degli Albanesi.

"fixed in the Venetian fashion." The beamed ceiling, far less costly than coffering – unadorned wood in St. Ursula's room and gilded and painted in Ser Nicolò's – was probably more typical of most Venetian homes.

Oriental carpets were frequently cited in inventories. They might be placed on the cold tile floor, as in Ursula's bedchamber, or used as table covers. In St. Anne's room, a carpet with a red and green pattern is draped over a low partition to create a bench for sitting. Signs of taste and wealth, such carpets were not local products, but were imported from the east. During Carpaccio's time, most of them came from Egypt and, less often, from Persia. They were to be had in various shapes and sizes: rectangular, round, and square, both with and without fringes. They featured both geometrical and figured patterns, and could be simple or quite elaborate. They were always colorful. On festive occasions they were draped over windowsills, emblems of a comfortable lifestyle spilling into the public sphere.

The bare walls are given architectural definition with a delicate linear design painted in reddish fresco. Aside from a plaque with a Hebrew inscription that placed the scene in biblical time, there are several other new elements in Carpaccio's painting: a row of small objects – jars, vases, and a candlestick holder – on the high ledge next to St. Anne's bed and a full set of dishes in the kitchen to the rear. We know from inventories that these were essential components of every well-furnished house. With the exception of textiles and carpets, which are particularly vulnerable to deterioration, many such objects survive today.

Had St. Anne been a young bride living in late fifteenth-century Venice, the ledge near her bed might have held a betrothal goblet (FIG. 92). A fine example in emerald-green glass features granular gilding and is decorated with two portrait medallions draped with garlands and flanked by cupids executed in enamels of various colors. The fashionably coiffed lady holding a bouquet is matched by a gentleman on the other side of the goblet who holds a scroll bearing the motto AMOR.VOL.FEE. (love requires faith). A token of love and marriage, the goblet is a very personal object. Its message would have been intended for an intimate audience: the lover and the beloved.

Different genres of art often shared the same images and motifs. The betrothal cup is a case in point, for the lovers depicted on the sides are clearly part of the same social world as Carpaccio's *Two Venetian Ladies on a Terrace*. Now in the Correr Museum in Venice, the painting is the lower half of a dismembered panel that was recently re-united, if only in a photo-montage, with a

92. Betrothal goblet, late 15th century. Enameled glass, height 8¾" (22.4 cm), diameter 4" (10.4 cm). British Museum, London.

Similar cups were made in milk glass called *lattimo*, using a technique that Venetian glassmakers developed in the mid-15th century in imitation of white porcelain imported from China.

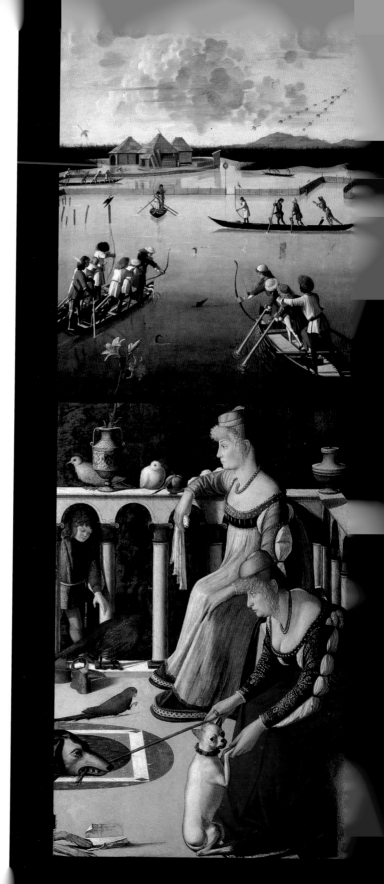

93. VITTORE CARPACCIO
Hunting in the Lagoon, c. 1495.
Oil on panel, 30 x 25" (75.4 x
63.8 cm). J. Paul Getty Museum,
Los Angeles, California.

The reverse of the Correr panel
(below) has been planed down, but
the reverse of the Getty panel is
painted with a *trompe l'oeil* image
of letters and notes stuck behind a
fictive ribbon tacked onto a board.
Both panels bear the marks of
hinges, suggesting the piece was
originally a door to a piece of
furniture or perhaps a shutter, and
that it was intended to be seen on
both sides.

94. VITTORE CARPACCIO
Two Venetian Ladies on a Terrace,
c. 1495. Oil on panel, 37 x 25¼"
(94 x 64 cm). Museo Civico Correr,
Venice.

Many elements in the scene are given
a dual symbolism in 16th-century
emblem books. The doves, though
companions of Venus, were symbols
of marital fidelity, as they were
thought to mate for life. The peahen,
sacred to Juno, was an emblem of
conjugal concord and fecundity. The
parrot, associated with amorous
activities, was also admired for his
ability to salute the Virgin with his
characteristic cry of *Ave*. As to the
orange, or *malus aureus*, its
associations include not only Venus
and the nuptial celebration of Juno
and Jove, but also the Virgin.

painting in the Getty Museum in California, known as *Hunting in the Lagoon* (FIGS 93 and 94). Technical analysis proves conclusively that the two paintings were originally a single panel (that probably extended further to the left), with the maiolica vase in the lower panel holding the lily that protrudes into the upper. With the two panels juxtaposed, Carpaccio's original intentions begin to emerge: to join the confined domestic recreation space of women to the more public recreation space of their male counterparts. The young boy, probably a page, provides a link – both visual and conceptual – between the two domains.

While some scholars have argued that the women are not respectable ladies at all, but Venetian courtesans waiting for customers, this view is surely a misreading of the work. Indeed, it is far more likely to be a celebration of marriage. The pair are dressed in the latest fashions worn by women of honor and sit decorously on an *altana* – the private rooftop terrace of their family palace. Even the most respectable patrician ladies in Venice – and Casola observed this with some relish – painted their faces and exposed their shoulders and a good amount of bosom. The dress and demeanor of Carpaccio's ladies represent the Venetian marital ideal of voluptuousness controlled by chastity or fidelity. The lady in the rear, the younger of the two, wears a pearl necklace, prohibited to prostitutes, and allowable in Venice only to noble brides. Her linen handkerchief is an emblem of her chastity. She is flanked by two vases, one holding lilies, long associated with purity, and the other myrtle, a symbol of marriage. The hound suggests vigilance, the lapdog fidelity.

Elegantly painted with the coat of arms of the ancient Preli family, the maiolica vase on the left end of the parapet would seem to offer a key to the identity of the sitters. However, with the patrician branch of the family having died out already in the twelfth century, it may be suggested that the blason pertains to a wealthy *cittadino* family, whose daughter is about to make a noble marriage. In any event, the vase introduces another element into our exploration of the Venetian home. Probably imported from one of the Umbrian hill towns that specialized in making tin-glazed earthenware, the depicted piece features a fish-scale pattern used on pottery made in Deruta. In Venice, the traditional ceramic of choice was incised slipware, involving a Byzantine technique in which earthenware is covered with a liquid white slip (or dilute clay) into which the decoration is scratched through to the darker clay before glazing.

95. WORKSHOP OF MATTEO D'ALVISE DA FAENZA(?) *Bella donna*, 1499. Maiolica jug (*boccole*), height 11¾″ (30 cm). Museo Civico, Bologna.

The maiolica technique was introduced to Venice at the end of the fifteenth century by craftsmen from Faenza. Early pieces made in Venice tended toward large, simple designs adapted from the slipware technique, such as a jug featuring the profile of a woman (FIG. 95). An example of a genre of pottery decoration called the *bella donna*, she embodies a type of female beauty that was particularly admired in that period: swept-back hair with a few provocative tendrils escaping; large protruding eyes; a plump face and a full bosom amplified by the swell of the vase. With an arrow piercing her milky white skin, the theme of the work was made clear by the *cartellino* bearing the word *Amore*. The date 1499 on the opposite side of the jug suggests that the piece was a gift relating to a specific event, such as a marriage or engagement. It was probably the product of a collaborative effort, with a potter from Faenza responsible for making the ceramic and a Venetian painter for adding its painted decoration. Although all clay had to be imported, Venice's policy of offering financial incentives to skilled artisans who relocated to the city helped the industry to develop quickly, and it was not long before Venetian maiolica-ware was considered equal to that of Faenza. In 1545 a decree was passed banning the importation of all foreign tin-glazed pottery except the distinctive Hispano-Moresque wares from Spain.

Relatively inexpensive, portable, and open to unlimited pictorial invention, ceramic painting was an ideal medium for making personal statements. In addition to objects of occasion, such as the betrothal cups and the vase painted with the family coat of arms, pieces decorated with classical motifs offered the opportunity to display the patron's humanistic learning and refined taste. A large plate in the Victoria and Albert Museum is a sophisticated example of a distinctive style of Venetian maiolica that emerged in the early years of the sixteenth century (FIG. 96). Painted with deep blue and white colors on a grayish-blue (*berettino*) glaze, it employs an *all'antica* triumphal decorative vocabulary that had enjoyed great popularity in a wide range of media in Venice since the late quattrocento. Here the allegorical figure of Abundance, attended by a cupid or winged putto, holds a cornucopia and reclines in the midst of a densely packed field of trophies. These include the spoils of war and the benefits of peace: armor, shields, and weapons; grotesque masks and musical instruments; horses

96. WORKSHOP OF DOMENICO DA VENEZIA(?) *Abundance Surrounded by Trophies*, c. 1540–50. Maiolica dish, diameter 18¹/₃" (46.5 cm). Victoria and Albert Museum, London.

Scattered among the trophies are several white placards, one inscribed with the name of the painter – J. Francesco Tertiarius – and another with *Venezia*. Venetian furnaces were the first to produce dishes of such generous dimensions.

and a slumbering dog. The border of the dish features four classicizing medallions, two containing male profile busts and two with reclining female nudes.

An Antique Ambience

Antiquity – that defining theme of the Renaissance – was itself an object to be collected. Sabba da Castiglione wrote of gentlemen who liked to "decorate their houses with antiques, such as heads, torsos, busts, ancient marble or bronze statues. But since good ancient works, being scarce, can not be obtained without the greatest difficulty and expense, they decorate it with the works of Donatello . . . or with the works of Michelangelo . . . [or other modern artists]." Sabba could have found no better example of a gentleman who adopted a cultivated lifestyle and fashioned his self-image through the acquisition of *anticaglie* and works of art than Andrea Odoni. A wealthy merchant, Odoni commissioned Lorenzo Lotto to portray him amidst his possessions (FIG. 97). The work was seen in Odoni's palace in 1532 by the writer Marcantonio Michiel who described it as a "portrait of Messer Andrea himself, in oil, half-length, contemplating some antique marble fragments."

Odoni lived in the *sestiere* of S. Croce on the Fondamenta (a street next to a canal) del Gaffaro, in a palace with a facade frescoed with mythological figures. Some of the pieces depicted in the portrait may well have been genuine ancient marbles as Michiel claimed, but others were surely copies. The sculpture in the left background, for example, is a reproduction of an over-life-size statue of *Hercules and Antaeus*, also in a fragmentary state, that was then in the Belvedere courtyard of the Vatican. In the background to the right are three nude statuettes that have not been linked to known antiques: another Hercules, identifiable from his lionskin and club; a kneeling female, probably a Venus or a Diana Bathing; and a putto or Cupid. The marble head at the lower right was probably a stucco cast of a bust of Hadrian listed in an inventory made in 1555 after Odoni's death. Propped against it is a female torso, possibly a Venus.

While several of these objects might well be Lotto's own inventions, Michiel also described numerous pieces of sculpture, both ancient and modern, as well as paintings, vases, and other works of art distributed throughout the house. Among these signs of taste and refinement were two illuminated books of hours; one of which may be the tiny leather-bound volume with ribbon ties that rests on the table with a handful of medals or coins in the painting.

Odoni, richly dressed in a voluminous charcoal-gray coat of a heavy material lined with wolf fur, wanted more than simply an accurate portrayal of his outward appearance. Engaging the viewer with a direct gaze, he proffers a statuette of Diana of Ephesus, a symbol of Nature or the Earth, contrasting her to the transience of human things as symbolized by the antique fragments. Extending his left hand in front of his heart in a gesture of sincerity, Odoni thus appears to profess his trust in Nature over the works of man.

More typically, the antique was brought into Venetian homes in a less ostentatious way. The chambers of St. Ursula and Ser Nicolò (see FIGS 79 and 86, pages 116 and 125) both reveal a comfortable assimilation of classical elements into the prevailing Gothic style. In Ser Nicolò's palace, pilasters, balustrades, and wainscoting are carved with foliate forms that include the lamps and sphinxes that were common elements in a generalized *all'antica* aesthetic. But, more tellingly, both rooms feature small nude

97. LORENZO LOTTO
Portrait of Andrea Odoni,
1527. Oil on canvas, 39³/₄
x 45″ (1 x 1.1 m). Royal
Collection, Hampton Court
Palace.

98. *Venus,* North Italian, end of the 15th century. Bronze, height 9″ (23.1 cm). Kunsthistorisches Museum, Vienna.

The statuette has long been attributed to Tullio Lombardo, but has no analogues within his oeuvre.

figurines, probably cast of bronze and gilded, that stand on the doorway lintels. By the last decade of the fifteenth century, an industry specializing in the production of antique-looking bronzes had developed in Padua and Venice.

A standing *Venus* crafted with truncated arms is an engaging example of one of these surrogate antiquities (FIG. 98). Cast of solid bronze, she was once painted with a blackish-brown lacquer but was probably never gilded. The worn-smooth surface, with the bare metal showing through in places, suggests that she did not spend all her time above a doorway. She was surely passed around between her owner and his guests, to be observed closely, handled, and, indeed, caressed. With elongated proportions and a hairstyle more contemporary than classical, she might be considered an antique "paraphrase" – albeit a conscious emulation – rather than a "forged antique." In any event, such anachronisms do not detract from an overall impression of balance and grace nor from her evocative power as a paradigm of classical beauty.

An Aesthetic of Escape

The world of classical myth also offered an avenue of escape from an ever more complex and challenging present. Humanists had learned this lesson well, making forays into the ancient past through its literature. The establishment of the printing industry in Venice in 1469 made such texts available to a far wider audience. During the next five years, over 130 editions would be printed in the city, a tally that would rise to around 3,500 by the end of the century. Early editions of classical texts were still informed by the manuscript tradition and were often decorated with illuminated frontispieces of stunning originality. They were particularly notable for their *trompe l'oeil* illusionism, a cognitive taste with roots in Paduan art, particularly in the circle of the young Mantegna.

Typically, they employed an architectural monument as a gateway to the text. A frontispiece to the life of Theseus in a copy of Plutarch's *Parallel Lives,* printed in Venice in 1478, thus features a large purplish-gray monument cut out like a picture frame to contain the first page of the text (FIG. 99). The surface of the monument is seemingly decorated with fictive grisaille carving in low relief: primarily floral arabesques on the left and top borders, trophies on the right, and a frieze of nymphs and satyrs on the base. Over this structure an elaborate apparatus of jeweled ornaments – encrusted with pearls, gems, and cameos in elaborate gold settings fashioned from classical motifs – appears to be suspended from tiny cords. At the top, two gold wreaths encircle tiny

99. GIROLAMO DA CREMONA (attrib.)
Frontispiece to Plutarch, *Parallel Lives*, printed in Venice by Nicolaus Jenson, 2 January 1478.
Parchment, 15³/₄ x 10¹/₂" (40.2 x 27 cm). Bibliothèque Nationale, Paris.

The volume carries the coat of arms of the Agostini, a Venetian merchant-banking family.

100. Titian(?)
Pastoral Symphony,
c. 1510. Oil on canvas,
43 x 54" (1.1 x 1.4 m).
Musée du Louvre, Paris.

scenes from Ovid: on the left, a group of sea creatures and on the right, Vulcan fashioning the wings of Cupid.

The monument sits in the unspoiled countryside of Arcadia, populated with satyrs and wild animals of forest and field: a lion and lioness and two pairs of deer who dwell together in a state of primeval harmony. With a lake with swans just visible at the right-hand side, this peaceful country is accessible to the reader only through the text.

By the first decade of the sixteenth century, Venetian artists would create a larger vision of Arcadia by bringing it into easel painting. The *Pastoral Symphony* is one of the masterpieces of the genre (FIG. 100). Its authorship is uncertain, with the majority of scholars attributing it to Giorgione or Titian or even to both artists. The subject of the work has also eluded a sure interpretation. Two young men, one elegantly dressed and the other clothed in the rough garments of a shepherd, are seated in the countryside. Flanking them are two voluptuous nude females, but the men look only at each other.

According to one proposal, the painting represents an attempt to offer a visual equivalent to the *Eclogues* of Virgil – a genre of pastoral poetry that enjoyed great popularity in the period and was imitated by Italian poets. The central idea was the excursion of the "highly cultivated young man" into the idyllic countryside of Arcadia where mortals mingled with gods. Not a place so much as it was a state of mind, Arcadia was neither only the real world nor only the pastoral one. It was a superimposition of both worlds.

As such it was distant enough to provide escape and close enough to be always accessible. Indeed, there are buildings in the distance, which remind us that the city is somewhere nearby. One of the major contributions of Venetian artists of this period was to transform this literary scenario into visual form.

In the *Pastoral Symphony*, the young men are making beautiful music, and the nymphs come out to listen. Thus the men *create* Arcadia – they bring it to life. The nymphs are not invisible. Rather, by being visible they encourage us to join in. And yet a melancholy tone pervades the work; there is a tacit acknowledgement that the peaceful arcadian world of Virgil is really unattainable.

The artist stresses the fictive quality of this world by his technique of painting. Loading his brush with thick oil paint, he applies it to a coarse canvas that has been primed with a dark ground. In some areas the globs of oil paint are deliberately left visible. All the figures are in harmony with the natural world, but while they are clearly distinguishable and are not totally absorbed into it, they are grounded in the paint itself. The artist becomes a poet with these paintings, and he wants us to see his hand.

Pastoral scenes were much favored by printmakers, and the genre soon expanded beyond Arcadia with scenes of rural life that brought it more completely into the present day. It is as if Venetian artists and patrons put down their copies of Virgil's *Eclogues* and opened up the *Georgics* – a poem dedicated to agriculture, with work now privileged over leisure. The shift from shady groves to expansive agrarian vistas can be discerned in the *Landscape with a Milkmaid*, a woodcut after a drawing by Titian (FIG. 101). The

101. TITIAN
Landscape with a Milkmaid, c. 1520–25. Woodcut from original sketch, 14³/₄ x 17″ (37.6 x 43.3 cm). National Gallery of Art, Washington, D.C.

scene includes not only a shepherd boy feeding his flock of sheep and goats, but also cattle and a woman milking a cow. Although the figures and barnyard animals are clustered in the foreground, the countryside of broad meadows and rocky outcroppings is an equal player in the composition. Like the *Pastoral Symphony*, it does not appear to be informed by a specific literary text, indeed, it comes close to a pure landscape; and yet the galloping horse in the middle ground and the eagle perched on a stump in the front plane – both missing from the original drawing – hint at a possible allegorical message. The poetic effect is grounded in Titian's essential naturalism, with a medley of textures and shapes bound together in an organic unity by means of a sensitive play of light, shadow, and texture.

The growing prominence of the rustic in Venetian art was paralleled by new initiatives in land reclamation in the Veneto. Already in the quattrocento, Venetians had sought refuge from a densely populated urban environment by purchasing farms on the mainland. In the century that followed, many families built or expanded villas, and participated in a distinctive culture of villa life, called *villegiatura*, with seasonal relocations from city to country living. Originally inspired by such classical writers as Pliny and Vitruvius, who extolled the benefits of a healthy country life, Venetians who developed their villas as working farms were given official support by the Venetian government, which sought to safeguard the food supply of the lagoon.

The rural aesthetic culminated in the paintings of Jacopo Bassano, an artist from the market town of Bassano, nestled in the foothills of the Dolomites northwest of Venice. He was particularly famous for his nocturnal scenes and paintings in which biblical events were set in the midst of country life. With his *Pastoral Landscape*, he is probably the first artist to translate the rustic environment of Titian's woodcut into paint (FIG. 102). The work has been called the earliest true landscape in sixteenth-century Italian painting. The hour is sunset; the mood is tranquil; the figures are absorbed in their own activities: preparing a simple meal, watering the sheep, sowing the last seeds before the sun goes down. The chromatic harmony of the work is based upon a tenebrous palette of earth colors. One can imagine no better escape from the material opulence of the Venetian palace and from the manmade character of its urban setting.

That such a work as Bassano's would find its place in a sumptuous domestic setting of kaleidoscopic color and intricate patterns is not surprising. Venetians throughout their history demonstrated a striking ability to incorporate the alien, and to make it their sensitive mouth, and pointed chin: features that are distinctive enough to suggest a specific, recognizable individual. His toga, broadly painted in *scarlatto*, is fastened at the neck with a meticulously rendered gold clasp. The calculated balance between abstraction and particularity comes close to a classical statement of the aristocratic ideal of the late quattrocento. Indeed, the sitter, with his self-confident demeanor and impassive gaze, is more an icon than a protagonist in a social transaction. As much a type as an individual, he represents his caste – the hereditary patriciate – as well as himself.

During the first half of the sixteenth century, Venetian sitters became more animated, if no less guarded. A more complex psychological dimension is already evident in the portraiture of Lorenzo Lotto. His *Young Man with a Lantern* (FIG. 105) engages the viewer in a manner that the self-possessed *Young Senator*, painted a generation earlier, might well have considered indecorous. His lips parted, as if he is about to speak, he gazes directly

105. Lorenzo Lotto
Portrait of a Young Man with a Lantern, 1506–08. Oil on panel, 16½ x 21" (42.3 x 53.3 cm). Kunsthistorisches Museum, Vienna.

106. TITIAN
Portrait of a Man in Blue,
c. 1512. Oil on canvas,
32 x 26" (81.2 x 66.3 cm).
National Gallery, London.

at the onlooker and seems to demand a response. The portrayal expresses an inner life of tension and suggests that aristocratic demeanor comes at a price. Rendered with an attention to surface detail that is characteristic of Northern European art, the painting betrays a debt to Dürer and was probably made immediately after the German artist's visit to Venice in 1506. Lotto retains the

146   *Caste, Class, and Gender*

109. JACOPO AND DOMENICO TINTORETTO
S. Giustina and the Treasurers, 1580. Oil on canvas,
7′1″ x 6′ (2.2 x 1.8 m). Museo Civico Correr (on deposit
from the Gallerie dell'Accademia), Venice.

The painting was originally paired with *St. Mark and the
State Chamberlains,* now in Berlin, and the two works once
flanked Carpaccio's *Lion of St. Mark* (see FIG. 54, page 81)
in the Palazzo dei Camerlenghi at the Rialto.

110. PARIS BORDONE
The Chess Players,
1550–55. Oil on canvas,
44 x 71¼" (1.1 x 1.8 m).
Staatliche Museen
Preussischer Kulturbesitz,
Berlin.

Several chess pieces
tumble onto the lap of the
man on the right,
suggesting that the
vicissitudes of fortune may
upset the most well-
established hierarchy.

depicted as individuals, with their faces well differentiated, they
are identified neither by name nor by emblem. Indeed, their
personal identities are not at issue here. As members of the permanent bureaucracy who ensured the smooth operation of the
government while their noble employers rotated in and out of
office, the secretaries were included in the painting as essential,
but subordinate, members of the body politic.

Paris Bordone's *The Chess Players,* a rare double portrait of
two gentlemen engaging in a game of chess, portrays another aspect
of patrician life (FIG. 110). The players sit in the garden of a
country villa, although the classical loggia to the rear would appear
to be more a product of the artist's fancy than an existing struc-

ture. Behind two men engaged in conversation at the far left, a falconer is visible inside the loggia. Under a tree in the right background, a group of four ladies is seated on the grass around their own chessboard, while at a table nearby a group of four men play at cards, an activity that was considered a distinctly lower form of entertainment and often censured. The simplest reading of the work would define it as a straightforward genre portrait, aiming to commemorate the pair in the foreground in an aristocratic activity known to exercise the rational faculties and praised for its capacity to chase away boredom. With the open-air setting, it might also be seen as a sophisticated culmination of the taste for the countryside that had emerged in the early years of the century.

Yet the scene may not be as detached from urban life as would appear at first glance. As one scholar has observed, a further key to interpreting it may be found in the *Libro di giuocho di scacchi*, a thirteenth-century treatise on chess written by a Dominican monk. Printed in Florence in 1493 and in Venice in 1534, it circulated widely and could well have been known to Bordone or to his patron. The subtitle of the Florentine version – "on the customs of men and the offices of nobles" – is prefaced in the Venetian edition with an additional explanatory phrase: "A new work which teaches about the true government of men and women of every degree, state, and condition."

In the treatise, the game of chess is presented as a political allegory of the civil life, with the chessboard itself a metaphor of the well-ordered state in which each piece has its correct role and place. At the top of the hierarchy are the "noble chess pieces": the king, queen, and knights who stand for themselves, along with the castles as "vicars of the king" and the bishops who denote the judges and assessors. Below this upper stratum are the "common chess pieces" or pawns, who represent the popular classes, from notaries and medical doctors down to tavernkeepers and manual laborers. The arrangement of the pieces on the board stresses the interdependence of the orders: "it should be known that the commoners are placed in front of the nobles, because the commoners are in a certain way the crown of the nobility."

In Bordone's painting, the bearded player on the right holds a castle in his hand and moves to checkmate his younger opponent, very likely his own son. In so doing, he instructs him on his role in "the true government of men and women of every degree, state and condition." Following this line of argument, the figures in the background become more than just a supporting cast for the portrait of a comfortable lifestyle. Rather, they represent the idle pleasures that the young man should put aside as he embarks upon a life of public service, the pre-ordained civic role of every Venetian patrician adult male.

The Feminine Ideal

A woman's role in Renaissance Venice was another matter altogether. She had only one place in official public life: as an adornment of the city. On most ceremonial occasions, women were, indeed, part of the spectacle, but primarily as escorts for noble visitors and as viewers who filled the windows of the *piano nobile*. In each case they were both subject and object: whilst part of the crowd of spectators who were necessary for any ceremonial event, they were also ornaments to be seen. Sanudo wrote: "The women are truly most beautiful; they go about with great pomp . . . and when some grand lady comes to Venice, they go out to meet her with 130 and more women, adorned and dressed with jewels of the greatest value and quality." The sumptuousness of their apparel and the costliness of their jewelry were thus not just visible signs of the individual wealth of their husbands; they were also to be understood as emblems of the wealth and power of the city of Venice itself.

Female portraiture developed along the same lines as portraits of men. Lotto's *Portrait of a Lady* represents the culmination of the quattrocento tradition of veristic, "topographical" portraiture that sought to "map" an individual's features (FIG. 103, page 143). With her auburn hair pulled back and tamed by a confining snood, the sitter is almost certainly a married woman of unimpeachable respectability – indeed, a veritable icon of the virtuous matron. Her direct gaze bespeaks an absence of guile, and the veil covering the shoulders of her fashionably low-cut gown attests to her modesty. The dark background projects her forward as she addresses the viewer, whether male or female, in a visual dialogue as an equal participant who has nothing to hide.

With Giorgione's *Laura*, painted around the same time, the individual portrayal of women in Venice moves into a new phase. Now the viewer is struck by the sitter's evasiveness and sensuality more than by her forthright character (FIG. 111). Indeed, the sitter represents a new vision of female beauty. Since the seventeenth century she had been identified with Petrarch's beloved, the virtuous Laura, because of the laurel branch behind her. More recently, scholars have held that her bare breast could not be a sign of virtue, but rather of wantonness, and that she must be one of the courtesans for which Venice was so famous. However, a recent study proposes that the debate about Laura's profession – or lack thereof – misses the mark and argues that the most interesting question here is not who or what the woman was, but how she is presented. Laura grasps the lapel of her coat, but the direction of her gesture is ambiguous. Whether she is concealing or revealing herself is unclear, but the point is that *she* is in control and able to determine the viewer's degree of access. As to the coat itself, it is a gendered garment. It would have been part of a man's wardrobe in that period, for women wore cloaks or shawls and not coats as outer garments. The artist has thus set up an opposition between a nude female body and a masculine public garment. The result is a subtle eroticization based upon a deliberate ambiguity.

111. GIORGIONE
Laura, 1506. Oil on canvas over wood, 16 x 13"
(41 x 33.5 cm). Vienna, Kunsthistorisches Museum.

The only clue to the patronage of the work is an inscription on the back of the painting. It states that Giorgione completed it on 1 June 1506, having painted it at the request of a "messer Giacomo" about whom nothing further is known.

The laurel branch is surely a metaphor, but again the meaning is elusive. While it may well have referred to the name of the sitter, laurel was also associated more broadly with poets and poetry. Petrarch's Laura was his creation, and laurel was an emblem of her chastity, just as it was an emblem of his poetic genius. Whether or not Giorgione's sitter wrote poetry is unknown, but her gesture could well be a metaphor for the activity of the poet, for he, too, conceals and reveals himself. And yet, self-revelation, whether physical or intellectual, was not considered seemly in a woman. Indeed, Laura's ambiguous gesture – at once threatening and exciting – was surely a gesture of seduction toward the male viewer. Though dangerous, the gesture is, however, tempered by Laura's sensuality. An intentional juxtaposition of textures heightens our sense of her physical presence, with her smooth breast caressed by the fur collar on her coat and encircled by a filmy veil. Her hair is pulled back severely, but wispy tendrils escape from it. So she is "just a woman."

The visual address of this work thus depends on a play of ambiguities and contradictions. As such, it would have challenged traditional views about female behavior. Women had long been judged by the single standard articulated by Ludovico Dolce: "But in a woman one does not look for profound eloquence or subtle intelligence, or exquisite prudence, or talent for living, or administration of the republic or justice, or anything else except chastity." At least in theory, there was no room for ambiguity. However, a new role was being explored by some women in this period: the courtesan. Unmarried, often well educated, literate, and musically gifted, courtesans began to move around the public spaces of Venice, while respectable women watched life from the windows of the *piano nobile* of the family palace. According to the best estimates, there were around ten thousand courtesans in the city – perhaps ten percent of the population – during the period when Giorgione painted *Laura*. What was particularly troubling about the courtesan was not her sexual morality as such, but her autonomy and independence. So Giorgione's multivalent portrait may well have been an inspired response to the ambiguity of a new middle ground for women who were neither ladies nor common prostitutes. We are reminded of the role of art as a mediating device between the ideal and the real state of affairs in a society, between traditional attitudes and new social categories.

Giorgione opened the way to a new genre of female portraiture in which the identities of the sitters are equally indeterminate. The sculptor Simone Bianco (doc. 1512–d. after 1553) soon translated the concept into marble with his *Bust of a Young Woman* (FIG. 112). Striking a careful balance between the ideal and the particular, the sculptor followed the classicism that Giorgione had applied to painting. Skillful carving renders the maiden's flesh seemingly soft and malleable and her chemise of a gossamer lightness. There is also a play between the prestige of the antique and fashions of the present. While classical nudity could have provided the original inspiration for revealing the maiden's bare breast, her chemise is contemporary Venetian. However, here the sitter is more a passive object of display than an independent agent who plays a role in her own self-presentation. Her dreamy expression suggests surrender and a sensuality that gains its power from its lack of definition.

112. SIMONE BIANCO
Bust of a Young Woman,
early 16th century. Marble,
height 17″ (43 cm).
Skulpturengalerie, Berlin-
Dahlem.

The sitter's expression
derives from Tullio
Lombardo's sculpted
portrayals of women in
the 1490s. Bianco made
a number of portrait busts
in both marble and bronze.
Those of males were
typically clothed in
antique togas.

113.   PALMA VECCHIO
Portrait of a Woman (La Bella), c. 1520.
Oil on canvas, 37½ x 31½" (95 x 80 cm).
Fundación Colección Thyssen-Bornemisza, Madrid.

The painting was once attributed to Titian because
of the sitter's resemblance to the sumptuously
dressed figure in his *Sacred and Profane Love*, but
the style is that of Palma. The letters on the parapet,
AM.B / N D, have not been deciphered.

Palma Vecchio's *Portrait of a Woman*, now known as *La Bella*, has an even more fluid character (FIG. 113). It may be asked whether this is a true and proper portrait of a sentient being or an image of ideal femininity. La Bella's flawless white skin and delicate features are complemented by the elaborate arrangement of her dark golden hair. With one plump hand caressing the ringlets that cascade over her right shoulder and the other grasping a box filled with jewelry, she might be seen as a *Vanitas* figure – an allegory of vanity. As with *Laura*, her degree of respectability cannot be fixed with certainty. Although she is expensively clothed in a sumptuous gown of red and blue silk, her voluminous sleeves are pulled down to expose her chemise. If we compare her to Lotto's *Portrait of a Lady* we immediately see how much more approachable – and touchable – she appears to be. Although confined behind a parapet and thus inaccessible, she invites a lingering examination. She too looks out at the viewer, but from an angle that blunts the intensity of her gaze. Her lips parted, she seems about to respond to the spectator who would possess her, if only visually. Indeed, Palma – like Giorgione – makes a direct appeal to the sense of touch with a whole range of textures: the soft hair, the plump shoulders that seem all the more bare by contrast to the filmy camisole, the huge taffeta sleeve whose crisp texture gives it a faceted quality, the heavy quilted sleeves, the hard edges of the parapet in front and the pillar in the background. But much of the erotic power of this work lies in its restraint, for the lady is more than just a body. There is intelligence in her gaze, and Palma maintains a sensitive equilibrium between suggestion and invitation.

Like Giorgione's *Laura*, Palma's sitter may well have been a courtesan, but here too the ambiguity remains, and it is probably intentional. A similar fluidity is true of many of Titian's portraits of women, such as his *Lady in a Blue Dress*, also known as *La Bella* (FIG. 114). Her costume and demeanor are characteristic of the growing formality of Venetian life just a generation later than Palma's more intimate *La Bella*. Adorned with a simple gold

114. TITIAN
Lady in a Blue Dress (*La Bella*), 1536. Oil on canvas, 39¹/₂ x 29¹/₂" (100 x 75 cm). Florence, Pitti.

chain necklace and decorously encased in a heavy gown of embroidered blue-green satin that flattens her bosom, she would appear to be the image of aristocratic propriety and perhaps the portrait of a noble wife; and yet the evidence suggests otherwise. The same sitter seems to have been the model for several of Titian's paintings of nudes, and this particular work was in his studio when Francesco della Rovere, the Duke of Urbino, wrote to his agent in Venice, asking him to buy "the portrait of that lady in the blue dress." The letter offers clues to contemporary attitudes about these paintings of beautiful women. That the canvas was in the artist's shop and available for purchase, along with the duke's implicit acknowledgement that the identity of the sitter was unknown to him and of no particular interest, suggests that it was not commissioned by a patron to portray a specific individual. Furthermore, the magnificent dress seems to have been as important as the sitter to the prospective buyer.

In all likelihood, many such paintings were made as objects of contemplation. They were not portraits in the modern sense – that is, visual commemorations of specific individuals – but portraits only in a conceptual sense, albeit with the features of a real living woman. Neo-platonic ideas expressed by the Venetian poet, Pietro Bembo, in the fourth book of *The Courtier* written by Baldesar Castiglione, provided a rationale for the appreciation of such images by the admiring male viewer: "By the ladder that bears the image of sensual beauty at its lowest rung, let us ascend to the lofty mansion where heavenly, lovely, and true beauty dwells, which lies hidden in the inmost secret recesses of God, so that profane eyes cannot behold it." As physical embodiments of the abstract idea of perfect beauty these painted and sculpted images of Venetian beauties could thus serve as the essential first step toward the contemplation of the divine.

The Cult of the Family

And yet, however prominent the courtesan may have been in Venetian public life, most women were destined to become wives and mothers or to enter convents. With the family the ideal – indeed, the fundamental – unit of civic life, portraiture was also used to commemorate familial relationships.

The Freschi were a most respectable *cittadino* family, whose male members enjoyed brilliant careers in the state bureaucracy. During the course of the fifteenth century, they began to compile a chronicle of family events: marriages, births, christenings, and deaths; dowry contracts; and significant career assignments. Around

115. *Zaccaria Freschi and Dorothea Zaccaria*, from the *Cronaca di famiglia Freschi*, c. 1500. Illuminated manuscript. Biblioteca Nazionale Marciana, Venice.

Dorothea died in 1500 giving birth to her tenth child, a tragic event that was duly recorded in the chronicle. Her untimely death – she would only have been in her mid-thirties at the time – may have provided the occasion for the illumination of the manuscript.

1500, the parchment manuscript was illustrated with a series of six miniatures that provided a visual document of marriages over three generations. Zaccaria Freschi, whose father and grandfather were both depicted with their respective wives, appears with Dorothea Zaccaria, whom he married in 1486 in a lavish wedding with "a large number of eminent men, all opulently dressed" in attendance (FIG. 115). The daughter of an admiral of the Arsenal, a high-ranking *cittadino* office, she brought with her a dowry of 850 ducats. While her husband Zaccaria wears the red toga allowed to a secretary of the Council of Ten, Dorothea's dress and hairstyle are similar to those seen in Carpaccio's painting of *Two Venetian Ladies* (see FIG. 94, page 131).

Both husband and wife are accompanied by the coats of arms of their respective families, acknowledging that a marriage is the joining together of two lineages. And yet, at marriage a woman

116. TITIAN
The Vendramin Family before the Reliquary of the True Cross, 1543–47. Oil on canvas, 6′9″ x 9′10½″ (2.1 x 3 m). National Gallery, London.

Behind Andrea are his oldest son Leonardo, already a bearded twenty-year-old when the painting was probably begun, and Bartolo (age fifteen), Francesco (fourteen), and Luca (thirteen). The more lively younger sons were on the opposite side in front of the altar: Federigo (eight), who holds a dog, Filippo (nine), and Giovanni (eleven).

becomes part of her husband's genealogy while bringing to him links from the male members of her own natal family. The equivalence granted to women in the Freschi chronicle is unusual and may be explained by the family's *cittadino* status. The patrician caste, by contrast, was perpetuated by a patriarchal system wherein nobility was inherited only through the male line. While patricians were careful to keep records of their family trees, they generally did not cite the first names of the brides who married into the family. In a typical patrician genealogy, Dorothea would have been listed only as "the daughter of Antonio Zaccaria."

The central importance of the male lineage to the patriciate is eloquently expressed in Titian's painting, *The Vendramin Family before the Reliquary of the True Cross* (FIG. 116). The work was listed in an estate inventory as "a large picture in which are portrayed the miraculous cross with ser Andrea Vendramin with seven sons and messer Gabriele Vendramin, with its ornament of gold, made by the hand of ser Titian." Andrea and Gabriele were brothers, descendents of the Andrea Vendramin who was Guardian Grande of the Scuola di S. Giovanni Evangelista in 1369, when the confraternity had received the relic of the True Cross from Philippe de Mezières, the Grand Chancellor of Cyprus – a high civil official who served under the king of the island. This early Vendramin also took part in one of the miracles for which the True Cross would become famous. The event was commemorated by Gentile Bellini in *The Miracle of the Cross at the Bridge of S. Lorenzo* (see FIG. 82, page 120). Titian's later depiction of Gabriele and Andrea Vendramin, along with Andrea's sons, in attitudes of pious devotion to the True Cross, thus refers by implication to a distinguished family history and to the special relation to the divine that the Vendramins had enjoyed through the centuries.

Significantly, Andrea – the bearded figure in the foreground dressed in red senatorial robes – is portrayed with his seven sons, but not with the seven daughters who are recorded in the sources. The white-bearded Gabriele Vendramin, though set further back in the scene, holds the place of honor in the center of the canvas. He was a cultivated man who gathered around him the leading intellectuals and artists of the city. In addition to a renowned art collection that included Giorgione's *Tempest* and the drawing-book of Jacopo Bellini now in the British Museum, he had acquired a distinguished collection of antiquities and housed them in a "*camerino delle anticaglie.*"

Titian's composition is a masterful solution to the problem of portraying no less than nine figures in a single scene, while preserving the individual character of each of them. Adapting the traditional formula of procession and arrival that had long been used for votive paintings, he substitutes the reliquary of the True Cross for the holy figures that would normally be located at one side. But he avoids the frieze-like arrangement that is typical of such scenes and gives the composition depth and rhythm by placing Gabriele on the altar staircase in the center and clustering the figures in groups to each side of him.

The colors are varied and carefully arranged to unify the entire pictorial field. Against the dominant ambient colors of the cloudy soft-blue sky and the buff-colored altar, Gabriele and his six youngest nephews – all dressed in black – provide a stable armature against which the red costumes of the other figures are contrasted. While the rich dark-red of Andrea's robe is heightened by the satiny rose-hued garments of his son Leonardo behind him and by the pinkish stole draped over Gabriele's right arm, it is subdued by the brilliant red stockings of little Federigo who sits on the steps opposite.

In his will, written in 1548, a year after his brother Andrea's death, Gabriele left his art collection to his nephews and, in a classic statement of the patrician ethos, gave them the following advice:

117. PAOLO VERONESE
Livia da Porto Thiene with her Daughter Porzia,
c. 1556. Oil on canvas, 82 x
47¼″ (2 x 1.2 m). Walters
Art Gallery, Baltimore.

Livia is sumptuously dressed in a rose-red gown with a matching coat of satin lined with tawny snow-leopard. A marten's fur with an enamel and gold head is draped over her arm.

118. PAOLO VERONESE
Giuseppe da Porto with his Son Adriano, c. 1556. Oil on canvas, 81½ x 54″ (2.1 x 1.4 m). Collezione Contini Bonacossi, Florence.

In the course of your lives you should follow those three things through which you can glorify your family and your country. The first is that you master navigation and that you put all your mind to the study and mastery of naval warfare; the second is that you do not abandon the study of letters; the third is that you take up the trading of merchandise and never leave debts unpaid.

In contrast to Titian's *Vendramin Family*, Veronese's pendant portraits of an aristocratic couple in Vicenza accorded decidedly equal treatment to the portrayal not only of husband and wife, but also of son and daughter: *Livia da Porto Thiene with her Daughter Porzia* and *Giuseppe da Porto with his Son Adriano* (FIGS 117 and 118). Indeed, their marriage in 1545 would have been seen as a brilliant match uniting two distinguished clans. Giuseppe was a wealthy nobleman and a knight of the Holy Roman Empire, while Livia was the daughter of one of the city's leading families. Full-length pendant portraits of married couples had recently become

fashionable in Verona and Vicenza, but they never took hold in Venice. The prominence enjoyed by Terraferma wives in family portraiture may derive from feudal traditions and more liberal inheritance rights accorded daughters.

Veronese's portraits were probably commissioned to flank a window in a new family palace designed by Palladio that was completed in 1552. Assuming a common light-source, Livia's painting would have been on the left, with her glance directed toward her husband while Porzia looks intently at the viewer with child-like candour from the security of her mother's protective embrace. The relationship to the beholder is reversed in the other painting. Here it is the father, Giuseppe, who addresses the viewer, while his son Adriano gazes fondly back at his little sister. Looked at together, the portraits celebrate dynastic values, as well as the genuine affective bonds of the conjugal family.

Bernardino Licinio (c. 1490–c. 1550), a Venetian-born artist whose family came from the Terraferma city of Bergamo, portrayed the family of his older brother Arrigo, also a painter (FIG. 119). A Latin inscription, probably added later by Bernardino's nephews, documents the artist's intentions and attests to his authorship: "Here Licinio portrayed his brother with all his family and thereby prolonged life for them with their image, for himself with his art." And yet, while the inscription emphasizes patriarchy,

119. BERNARDINO LICINIO *Portrait of Arrigo Licinio and his Family*, c. 1535– 40. Oil on canvas, 46½ x 65″ (1.2 x 1.7 m). Galleria Borghese, Rome.

The painting is inscribed in the upper right-hand corner: *EXPRIMIT HIC FRATREM TOTA CUM GENTE LYCINUS / ET VITAM HIS FORMA PROROGAT ARTE SIBI.* The artist's signature is below: *B. LYCINII OPUS.*

the painting itself celebrates maternity. Placing his brother in the left background, Bernardino made his sister-in-law, Agnese, a veritable icon of motherhood. Holding an infant and surrounded by five sons and a daughter, she is the centerpiece of the painting. The ages of her children, spanning nearly twenty years, attest to a life of frequent pregnancies.

The oldest son, Fabio, holds a statuette of the Belvedere Torso, one of the prize antiquities of the papal collection in the Vatican palace; trained as a goldsmith, he would later become an etcher. Directly in front of him is his younger brother Giulio, who offers his mother a basket of roses; he later became a painter and worked as Bernardino's assistant. Camillo, standing between his parents, was to become a famous physician. The other children do not appear in later documents and may have died in childhood. The portrait affirms the central role of the mother in an artisan family and celebrates the individuality of each of its members.

Several decades later, Veronese painted what might be considered the most comprehensive image of family solidarity of the Venetian cinquecento. The *Presentation of the Cuccina Family to the Madonna* derives its format from votive paintings hung in public offices and is unusually large for a private commission (FIG. 120). Flanked by an angel and SS. John the Baptist and Jerome, the Madonna and Child are seated in front of a sumptuous brocade curtain at the left end of the canvas in a holy space demarcated by a pair of monumental marble columns. Kneeling on the steps to the right of the columns in decidedly worldly space are Alvise Cuccina and his wife Zanetta, surrounded by six sons and their daughter, Marietta. The infant held by the nurse at the far right would have been little Zuanbattista, who was born in late 1571 or early 1572.

In accordance with Venetian custom intended to preserve the patrimony, Alvise's two brothers remained unmarried and would have been part of his family. Indeed, they too are participants in the scene. Zuanantonio, who stands above Alvise, looks out from behind a pillar; but Antonio, kneeling on the right, plays a more prominent role, for he is accorded special attention by the three theological virtues who present the family to the Christ child. Faith, a queenly figure clothed in white who holds a chalice, takes him by the hand; Hope bows her veiled head and gestures toward the holy figures; and Charity, wearing a

120. PAOLO VERONESE *Presentation of the Cuccina Family to the Madonna,* 1571. Oil on canvas, 5'5¾ x 13'7¾" (1.7 x 4.2 m). Staatsgalerie, Dresden.

Veronese painted three other large canvases (also in Dresden) for the Cuccina palace (now the Palazzo Papadopoli): *The Adoration of the Magi, The Wedding Feast at Cana,* and *The Road to Calvary.*